P9-AQR-410

Snap Judgment

Snap Judgment

When to Trust Your Instincts, When to Ignore Them, and How to Avoid Making Big Mistakes with Your Money

David E. Adler

Vice President, Publisher: Tim Moore
Associate Publisher and Director of Marketing: Amy Neidlinger
Executive Editor: Jim Boyd
Editorial Assistant: Myesha Graham
Development Editor: Russ Hall
Operations Manager: Gina Kanouse
Digital Marketing Manager: Julie Phifer
Publicity Manager: Laura Czaja
Assistant Marketing Manager: Megan Colvin
Cover Designer: Alan Clements
Managing Editor: Kristy Hart
Project Editor: Anne Goebel
Copy Editor: Bart Reed
Proofreader: Apostrophe Editing Services
Indexer: Lisa Stumpf
Senior Compositor: Jake McFarland
Manufacturing Buyer: Dan Uhrig

This book is sold with the understanding that neither the author nor the publisher is engaged in rendering legal, accounting or other professional services or advice by publishing this book. Each individual situation is unique. Thus, if legal or financial advice or other expert assistance is required in a specific situation, the services of a competent professional should be sought to ensure that the situation has been evaluated carefully and appropriately. The author and the publisher disclaim any liability, loss, or risk resulting directly or indirectly, from the use or application of any of the contents of this book.

FT Press offers excellent discounts on this book when ordered in quantity for bulk purchases or special sales. For more information, please contact U.S. Corporate and Government Sales, 1-800-382-3419, corpsales@pearsontechgroup.com. For sales outside the U.S., please contact International Sales at international@pearson.com.

Company and product names mentioned herein are the trademarks or registered trademarks of their respective owners.

ISBN-10: 0-13-714778-3
ISBN-13: 978-0-13-714778-6

Pearson Education LTD.
Pearson Education Australia PTY, Limited.
Pearson Education Singapore, Pte. Ltd.
Pearson Education North Asia, Ltd.
Pearson Education Canada, Ltd.
Pearson Educación de Mexico, S.A. de C.V.
Pearson Education—Japan
Pearson Education Malaysia, Pte. Ltd.

Library of Congress Cataloging-in-Publication Data

Adler, David E.

 Snap judgment : when to trust your instincts, when to ignore them, and how to avoid making big mistakes with your money / David E. Adler.

  p. cm.

 ISBN 978-0-13-714778-6 (hbk. : alk. paper) 1. Investments—Psychological aspects. 2. Investments—Decision making. 3. Finance—Psychological aspects. 4. Finance—Decision making. I. Title.

 HG4515.15.A35 2009

 332.024—dc22

Contents

Acknowledgments ix

About the Author .xi

Introduction 1

Part I: **The Psychology of Financial Decisions**

Chapter 1.   Money Is a Drug 15

Chapter 2.   Buy High, Sell Low: The Basic Instinct
              Driven Error of Investing 21

Chapter 3.   More About Stocks: Dividends—Behavioral
              Ways to Play the Dividend Game 27

Chapter 4.   Bonds: Malign Neglect 33

Chapter 5.   The Psychology of Why People
              (Used to) Hate Annuities 39

Chapter 6.   The Psychology of Selecting Mutual Funds .47

Chapter 7.   Building Your Portfolio the Behavioral
              Economics Way 55

Chapter 8.   Risk Tolerance and Investing 61

Chapter 9.   Deconstructing Stock Analysts 67

Chapter 10.   Value Investing: Behavioral Origins 73

Chapter 11.   Timing Stocks 77

Chapter 12.   Momentum 83

Chapter 13.   The Ultimate Anomaly: Trusting Your
              Gut in Finance 91

Part II: **The Track, the Stock Market,
                    and Other Types of Gambling**

Chapter 14.   Let's Talk about Linda: More About Our
              Intuition 95

Chapter 15.   Why Investors Bet on Long-Shot Horses . .109

Chapter 16.   Gambling Continued: Stories We Tell
              Ourselves 113

Chapter 17.   Fourth and Ten: Insights into NFL
              (and Corporate) Decision Making 119

Chapter 18.   Football Stories, Continued:
              The NFL Draft 125

Chapter 19.   The Inner Game of Tennis, Revisited . . .131

Chapter 20.   How to Make Money Gambling:
              Behavioral Insights 135

Chapter 21.   The Truth About Coin Tosses:
              They Aren't Fair .143

Part III: **Personal Decisions: Personal Safety,
                    Personal Finance, and Health Choices**

Chapter 22.   Personal Security: Assessing Danger 151

Chapter 23.   Credit Card Stories: Beating Your
              Credit Card Charges Using Behavioral
              Economics 155

Chapter 24.   Snap Judgment and Social Security:
              When Should You Claim It? 163

Chapter 25.   How Patients Think Irrationally 167

Chapter 26.   Health Insurance Decisions 173

Chapter 27.   Car Accidents 177

Part IV: **CEO Behavior**

Chapter 28.   Strategic "Styles" .183

Chapter 29.   CEO Hubris 189

Chapter 30.   Firing CEOs 195

Chapter 31.   Using CEO Behavior for Investing 197

Chapter 32.   Wall Street CEOs 199

Part V: **Psychology and the Credit Crisis**

Chapter 33.   Background: Bubbles and
                When They Explode 207

Chapter 34.   Fear and Loathing in Ft. Lauderdale 213

Chapter 35   Follow the Mortgage 219

Chapter 36.   Risky Business: Bank Runs 229

Chapter 37.   Euphoria, Fear, and Economics: A
                Psychological Autopsy of the Crisis 235

Part VI: **Conclusion: Debiasing**

Chapter 38.   How Not to Blink in the Face of
                Financial Panic .249

Chapter 39.   A Summing Up: Twilight of the Gods 261

                Index 265

Acknowledgments

I would like to thank the Summer Institute in Behavioral Economics at the University of Trento, Italy, and its organizers, visiting faculty, and students, who reminded me how vital economics can be. I don't know if it was the attitude or the altitude or some combination thereof, but discussing behavioral economics in classrooms and during hikes in the Dolomites was an immensely intellectually exciting experience.

Back at sea level, in New York and London, this book owes everything to Jim Boyd, my editor, who is a paragon of good decision making in every way imaginable; my production editor Anne Goebel and copy editor Bart Reed; Toby Butterfield and Lisa Digernes of Cowan, DeBaets, Abrahams & Sheppard; Marion Asnes, who read many drafts, and Vanessa Drucker, who read every draft.

Finally, a note about persistence. Most economists claim they can find almost no evidence of "persistence" by investment managers, meaning the ability to continuously beat the market. However, I was extremely "persistent" in tracking down economists and investment managers for their views and stories; there can be no doubt about that. Therefore, my message to Harry Markowitz, Andrew Lo, Joseph Stiglitz, Gary Loveman, Keith Stanovich, Meir Statman, Shane Frederick, Justin Wolfers, Kent Womack, David Romer, Steven Sass, Dan Fuss, Jeff Wurgler, Charles Plott, Robert Pelton, Rob Arnott, Theo Vermaelen, Lasse Pedersen, Dirk Jenter, Antoinette Schoar, my undisclosed "deep throat" at Lehman Brothers, Mark Schlesinger, Hyun Shin, Marcus Brunnermeier, Hersh Shefrin, Jeffrey Brown, Cade Massey, Susan Holmes, Jonathan Zinman, and everyone else I spoke to is this: If I overdid it, my apologies, and also my thanks. This book could not have been written without your time and guidance.

About the Author

David E. Adler's previous book, *Understanding American Economic Decline* (Cambridge University Press), coedited with the historian Michael Bernstein, was an anthology of essays by economic historians examining America's financial problems in a historical context. David Adler has written for *Barron's, Institutional Investor, The New Republic, Psychology Today,* and *Financial Planning,* where he is a contributing writer focusing on high net worth investing. He has a BA and MA in economics from Columbia and also studied graduate economics at New College, Oxford.

David Adler has also produced documentaries on art, American popular culture, and economics for the BBC and U.S. television. His documentary *Financial Insecurity: America's Crisis in Healthcare and Retirement* was shown on PBS stations in 2005. He is currently the recipient of a research grant from the CFA Institute Research foundation studying tax-aware investment techniques. He divides his time between New York's East Village and London.

Introduction: Second Thoughts About First Impressions

I can resist everything except temptation.
—Oscar Wilde

This book is about the psychology of financial decisions. It is about how our instincts and intuitive judgments intersect with financial markets, as well as other areas of contemporary life, to produce decisions that are not in our best interests. It argues that our "intuition," the psychological responses celebrated in books like *Blink*, may be a useful guide when falling in love, but when it comes to investing, fully trusting your gut is pretty much a disaster. It will only lead you astray when choosing a stock or predicting the end of a real-estate boom. Snap judgments and first impressions are poorly suited for calculating odds and probabilities, compounding interest, or forecasting the future behavior of the stock market.

This book examines decision making in many areas of finance, such as picking stocks, bonds, mutual funds, and health insurance, too. It looks at how gamblers misperceive odds, and ways both sports teams and corporations could improve their strategies through a better understanding of probabilities. It shows how we naturally extrapolate current financial trends into the future, causing us to become irrationally optimistic—or alternatively to panic and subject ourselves to doom-and-gloom scenarios. The finance industry is well aware of our intuitive errors when it comes to investing and knows exactly how to get us to make the wrong move.

The message of the book is a positive one, and also a pragmatic one. When it comes to investing, you can teach yourself to recognize your instinct-driven errors. This will allow you to temper your intuition, where appropriate, with more deliberate and also more informed thought. Through conscious effort we can resist the siren call of our gut instincts.

This book also comprehensively presents the most interesting recent findings of the rapidly growing field of behavioral economics, which draws on both psychology and finance. Some of the early ideas of behavioral finance are now widely known and are part of the mainstream of investment advice. But there is much more contemporary research that has not yet filtered out to a wider audience, and remains only in the hands of specialists. Whenever possible, I interviewed the creators of these newer ideas, to get it straight from the horse's mouth, or economist's mouth so to speak. Investors can profit from this new research, and I mean that literally. Keynes once compared the stock market to a beauty contest, where the goal was not to pick the contestant you found the most beautiful but instead to be able to spot the one everyone else was going to select. If you know how other investors judge stocks, think about markets, and are going to behave, that gives you an enormous leg up. This book discusses several persistent "anomalies," predictable departures from market efficiency, where through an understanding of investor psychology, rational investors can improve their chances of beating the market.

There is also a more ominous theme to the book. Relying only on intuition in finance—making the decision that seems right and *feels* right—can lead to very bad outcomes, not only for individuals but also for markets. These gut instincts, uncontrolled by self-regulation or government regulation, can give rise to huge financial bubbles. As we all know now, the U.S. spent the last decade or so in the grip of a mass euphoria of twin real-estate and credit bubbles. Individual investors and investment bankers made errors in judgment. The system, and the people in it, seemed to be in a sort of dream state during the bubble years. This was more than simple greed. Rational thought was in short supply. Few people worried about the possible fragility of the system itself. Rising markets made investors complacent, stifling good judgment and decision making. Using gut instincts and intuitive perceptions for guidance, aided by dubious mathematical models that few explicitly questioned, no one saw the true dangers ahead, leading to a financial catastrophe.

Gut Instincts and Evolution

Cognitive psychologists and decision theorists believe we have two decision systems at our disposal. The most immediate, written about in Malcolm Gladwell's *Blink*, is very quick, based on first impressions. These are snap judgments that occur almost instantaneously in the blink of an eye, with little deliberation. The ability to make quick intuitive decisions is an evolutionary adaptation, according to evolutionary psychologists. It developed so humans could function in early environments. Speed in thinking was everything. When should you run from a mammoth? Or toward a mammoth, hoping to spear it for dinner? Pausing to deliberate in such a moment could literally kill you. The brain of early man needed to fire off answers to these questions in a split second.

More generally, evolutionary psychologists argue that our early brains evolved to make quick decisions for another reason: Early man needed to master his rapidly changing social environment. This was central to human development. Our cognitive capabilities are hardwired to interpret and understand social cues. These social mechanisms are still present in our brains and pervasively color all of our thinking, including our assessment and interpretation of abstract patterns with no human presence.

Today, there are certain areas of life where this quick thinking, human-oriented decision system—call it intuition—still works well. Understanding the contemporary social environment is one of them: Is the colleague from the cube next door, that you are having lunch with, a friend? Enemy? Frenemy? Snap judgments rather than conscious deliberation may be your best guide.

Interpreting language cues, even when extremely subtle, is another area where you don't have to think too consciously to understand what is going on. People make inferences based on language and do so astonishingly fast. Take, for instance, the seeming compliment in the phrase, "Well, I liked your book," overheard in a conversation between writers. As opposed to reading it on the written page, listening to the delivery reveals this is not necessarily a compliment at all but instead could be meant as an insult. Emphasis on the word *I* conveys a hidden meaning, "Yes, maybe *I* did like it, but this was in contrast to everyone else. Everyone else hated it." An analytical or nonintuitive approach would miss the hidden dig. Similarly, artists undermine each other with the description, "She's a *competent* painter." The listener can infer this means nothing good, that the artist in question is mediocre and unimaginative.

Our intuition is also pretty good at recognizing how frequently things occur in nature. (Animals, in general, are good frequency detectors. They seem to uncannily forage in exactly the right place. They vary their hunting grounds in an evolutionarily determined, precise way so as to maximize caloric intake while minimizing caloric expenditure.) Our intuition can perform many other extraordinary feats: We are great at face recognition—we can pick out a face from a crowd of 10,000 people. We can easily sense the moods of other people.

These are all evolutionary mechanisms, high-speed inferences. And they work superbly well in areas with evolutionary precedent, areas that still resemble in some way the challenges facing early man, such as picking a mate, anticipating a rival's actions, or selecting what to wear. (A New York celebrity fur designer claims that the world's oldest profession is being a furrier!)

However, this system doesn't work well in situations that are different from those encountered by early man. To put it more formally, when the operating environment has shifted from what the system was designed for, our evolutionary adapted mechanisms are no longer effective. In these situations, relying only upon our gut instincts will lead to failure, fully predictable failure.

Investing is one of those areas.

A Second Way of Reaching a Decision

Try to solve the following simple math problem: A baseball bat and ball cost $1.10 in total. The baseball bat costs $1.00 more than the ball. How much does the ball cost?

The problem is not really a math problem, it's a psychological test. Because the answer, and our method of arriving at it, illustrates the limits of our intuition. If you are like most people, your immediate answer to the problem is the ball costs 10 cents. The majority of undergraduates at Princeton who were asked the question gave that answer. But that, of course, is the wrong answer ($0.10 + $1.10 = $1.20). The correct answer is the ball costs five cents. But to arrive at the correct answer, you probably had to pause for moment, for at least a beat, to think consciously rather than using your immediate intuition.

The fast and then the slow way of answering this simple math problem—each of which provides a different answer—illustrates that humans have at their disposal an additional method of thinking, a type of information-processing architecture other than intuition. Call it analytic intelligence or conscious decision making. This invokes rule-based decisions, nonsocial decisions that require abstract thought. This was the system you probably had to rely upon to answer the math question. Such thinking is time consuming, not immediate, and involves conscious reasoning. This analytical decision system is probably a more recent evolutionary adaption than intuition. Interpreting statistical information or probabilities, understanding legal arguments, and calculating interest rates call upon this more abstract type of reasoning.

Keith Stanovich is a psychologist at the University of Toronto who studies human development and reason. He is a world's expert at

researching the differences between both types of decision making—
intuitive and analytical. His experiments look at the way children
reach decisions in situations requiring use of probabilities and logic.
In one experiment, children are given the task of trying to choose a
white-colored marble from containers that have blue and white marbles in varying amounts. The containers vary in size. The biggest container has the smallest proportion of white marbles. Children relying
only on intuition, rather than probabilistic reasoning, tend to choose
the biggest container (with more "winning" white marbles but a
smaller proportion of winners) as the likeliest place to find the white
marbles, an incorrect answer. The general conclusion of his experiments is that cognitive ability is strongly associated with being able to
override intuition and instead using the harder-to-access analytic system.

There are no widely agreed upon names for these two systems.
Our intuitive, instinctive, automatic, experiential, heuristic, emotional, visceral, snap judgment–oriented, appetite-driven, or hot system is called by Stanovich "System 1." The analytical, rational,
reflective, deliberative, central-processing, or abstract system (all
common words to describe it) is termed "System 2" by Stanovich.
System 2 involves long drawn-out cognition. In System 1, answers are
arrived at in milliseconds. Think of the distinction as answers that
come from your gut (System 1) versus your mind (System 2).

Stanovich summarizes the difference between the two systems,
and why this difference is important: "System 1 gives ballpark answers.
But modern society requires precision beyond ballpark answers."

When there is no evolutionary precedent for a problem, intuition
isn't going to cut it. Contemporary life is filled with situations and
problems that must be dealt with both precisely and abstractly. The
ability to decontextualize and think abstractly is more important than
relying on social cues. Sometimes there are no social cues. Try arguing with your mutual fund after you've watched your 401(k) disappear
in the stock market decline. Or try appealing to the common sense of

your credit card company. In these circumstances, Stanovich points out, "We invariably find out that our personal experience, our emotional responses, our stimulus-triggered intuitions about social justice—all are worthless."

Our intuitive system has not evolved for these abstract problems, which is why we have so much trouble selecting a 401(k) investment, knowing when to sell a stock, choosing the best health insurance plan, compounding interest rates, assessing the risks of complex mortgage-backed "structured products," or dealing with probabilities and statistics in general. It's why we believed real estate could only go up—or after the crash, only go down. It's why investment bank CEOs, based on their decade-long success, began to think they could do no wrong. It's why we hire the wrong employee who seemed so charming at the job interview. It's why we underestimated the risks of credit markets and didn't see growing possibility of a systemic meltdown.

The real problem is when we exclusively use our intuitive system to guide us in what are in fact abstract situations. Predictable biases arise. The answers aren't even in the ballpark. Take, for example, the "gambler's fallacy." This is the belief that because a coin has come up heads many times in row, it is more likely to come up tails the next flip. But the coin has no memory. The outcome remains random, regardless of what happened in the past. Instead *we* remember, *we* imbue random outcomes with meaning, even with a sense of fairness, and mistakenly predict "tails." (For the surprising situations where coin flips may not be random, and in fact are subtly biased, see Chapter 21, "The Truth About Coin Tosses: They Aren't Fair.")

And this sort of fallacy is also true in the way we view the stock market. We see patterns or think narratives are at work where none exist. We in effect socialize stocks, treating inanimate objects as if they had human characteristics. If we paid a certain amount for a stock, we think it's only fair that we get at least that much back when we sell it, which might *feel* true, but has no bearing on the future direction of the price.

The dangerous intersection of our intuition and financial decision making has been studied in great detail by cognitive psychologists. Though not everyone is onboard Stanovich's evolutionary framework just yet, the field has agreed there are systematic biases in our intuitive thinking, which I describe in detail later in the book. In general, these mental rules of thumb, known as *heuristics*, simplify decision making. Though useful when we have to think quickly, they can lead to predictable errors when more abstract analysis is called for.

You can also make the opposite mistake: using analytical intelligence to solve what are essentially instinctual problems. In one famous jam experiment (there are actually several famous jam experiments in decision psychology), a group of participants were asked to rate jams using abstract dimensions: color, consistency, mouth feel. Another group was just asked which jam they *liked* the best. The group trying to use complex cogitation was thrown off; they could not reach a good operational judgment of what made for a good jam, unlike those who just chose the jam they liked. The conclusion is, you shouldn't over-think what you like in a jam.

Again, it is not every situation—very few in fact—where we need to override our intuitive system. Our intuition and abstract thought are not necessarily in conflict and may in fact support each other. However, in post-caveman life, there are many situations and decisions where our evolutionarily honed intuitive system is poorly adapted and doesn't serve us well. Stanovich's distinctions between the decision systems become crucially important in certain contexts where it can be extremely dangerous and self-injuring to be only guided by intuition.

The good news is you can teach yourself to check your intuition where necessary, to override your fundamental computational biases and use your analytical thought system instead. System 1 is our default, but through conscious effort, we can resist the temptation of listening to our gut, and instead make use of System 2. Airplane pilots do it all the time: They rely upon instruments to tell them if their plane is level rather than trusting their inner ears. The amazing fact is through learning and experience, cold, formal, analytical rules become automatic—second nature so to speak. If someone ever asks you again: "A baseball bat and ball cost $1.10 in total. The baseball bat costs $1.00 more than the ball. How much does the ball cost?" The correct answer of a nickel is now intuitive.

Making Better Financial Decisions

That people aren't always rational when it comes to financial decisions is clear, particularly after recent events. Everyone screwed up: sophisticated hedge funds and investment banks, as well as naive mortgage borrowers. The more interesting questions are: Why do we make these decisions, and to be more precise, when do we make them? Are they predictable? What can we do to make better financial decisions? How can we build a stronger financial system given how people behave?

The rest of this book describes ways to improve your decision making when it comes to *specific* issues in investing—and some areas in real life, too. Identifying circumstances where you should trust your gut versus situations where you need to do everything in your power to ignore it, is central to good decision making. The exact mechanism of how intuitive and analytical thought interact is unknown and is the subject of fierce debate among decision theorists. For Stanovich, the two types of decision systems can work together or in isolation, it all depends on what is being decided. Trusting your gut instinct is the way to go if the question has evolutionary precedent, such as "Do I recognize that face?" or "Do I love my spouse?" But if you are deciding which computer to buy, then an analytical approach is called for.

Financial decisions are more complicated. What makes investing so complex, as we shall see, is that although financial markets are primarily random and hence nonintuitive, not every manager's performance is random. Some are better than others at beating the market. And there are some stock market patterns you may be able to spot intuitively that I will discuss in the book. However, they are few and far between.

The recent real-estate and credit bubbles, followed by the liquidity crisis, are extreme examples of what can go wrong when we privilege feelings over reason, particularly in a setting with few regulations in place to save us from our own worst tendencies. The gyrations of the stock market are particularly tempting to intuitive interpretations, and this is where individual investors, if they rely solely on their intuition for guidance, can face the greatest peril. But as we will see in later chapters, gambling in Vegas, football strategy, horse racing, and even a tennis game can be improved through a bit more conscious deliberation. TARP bailouts, securitizing a mortgage, setting limits on leverage, rating a collateralized debt obligation, and deciding whether to let Lehman Brothers live or die could also benefit from relying on analytical thinking rather than snap judgments.

The first part of this book focuses entirely on financial decisions. It includes advanced techniques used by very sophisticated investors who attempt to beat the market through an understanding of investor psychology. It spells out why these strategies work, and how they work. The parts that follow look at intuitive mistakes we make in real life outside of investing—in sports and gambling decisions, as well as healthcare and credit card choices. The next section analyzes CEO behavior, particularly that of Wall Street CEOs during the crisis. The final chapters examine the financial crisis from a behavioral economics perspective. The book concludes with ways to improve decision making, leading to better investing.

Good financial decision making doesn't have to be complex or theoretical. You don't have to train yourself to become the financial equivalent of an airplane pilot—you don't have to fly on instruments alone and become a pure "quant." All you have to do is to think beyond your first impulse. Don't glaze over when facing a tough financial choice, or when presented with a supposedly unassailable computer model. Kick the tires of what's in front of you, and ask if the information and your response to it make sense. It really couldn't be simpler: When it comes to investing, have second thoughts about your first impressions.

Part I
The Psychology of Financial Decisions

1

Money Is a Drug

In the summer of 2008, Rob Arnott's research indicated there were problems ahead in the commodities boom. Arnott, founder of Research Associates, Inc., the giant Newport Beach-based money manager, is a quantitative investor as well as a contrarian who goes against the herd. His entire career has been built on finding ways to counter human emotions, including his own. His research but not his gut instincts told him that prices in commodities, including oil, had gone too far, and the future held more downside than upside.

This was not the conventional wisdom: Oil prices had surged by 300% between 2003 and 2007, and their climb upward seemed to only be accelerating. In 2008, prices crossed the once unthinkable $100 a barrel threshold, then $110, and finally brushed past $140 a barrel. Mainstream thinking held that the price increase was the result of changed fundamentals in the world economy. The newly awakened Chinese and Indian economies, with their nearly unquenchable thirst for raw materials, could only send the price of oil to higher and higher levels. Analysts who questioned if oil was in fact in the midst of an unsustainable price bubble were dismissed as bubble headed.

Arnott questioned his quantitative-based commodity. After all, the smart money, led by sophisticated institutional investors such as Harvard's endowment, continued to pour money into oil. The continuing rise in price seemed to reinforce the wisdom of their decision. As Arnott admits, "I looked for ways to tweak the models, to fix them because the models were missing the huge bull market in commodities. That is what my intuition told me." Arnott's intuition, which was in conflict with the models, was wrong. The models had been right.

The price of oil soon crashed, but not before Arnott had sold his position. As an investor, he has trained himself to listen to his intuition—only to then do the opposite. "I use intuition, but in a warped fashion," he says. If he feels comfortable about the direction his models are pointing him in, if they are in sync with his intuition, he immediately begins to worry.

He explains why so much of investing is nonintuitive: "The natural instinct is to follow others. As we were evolving on the plains of Africa, if everyone in the tribe starting running, you better start running. But in investing, if you act after everyone has starting running, you are catching the late end run of an asset and your timing will be atrocious." For most investors, doing what comes naturally means chasing trends, doing what everyone else is doing. But although this makes sense in other areas of life, it is not a wise strategy for investing.

The easiest way for an investor to overcome this vulnerability is simply to build a natural skepticism to natural instincts. You don't have to become a dogmatic contrarian—you just have to question your first impulse. Take, for example, a typical scene at a cocktail party. Someone brags about their fantastic investment. The natural reaction is to ask yourself if you are missing out on a great opportunity. The more skeptical and informed reaction should be to ask if the great past performance will continue into the future. Have you missed your window? Is it still attractive at current prices?

Arnott has trained himself to ask these counterintuitive questions when thinking about a new investment opportunity, and he feels everyone else can do the same. But he is merely one investor among many. And, the fact is, during the bubble years few investors showed this sort of skepticism—or any sort of skepticism. The entire world seemed intoxicated with money. It did seem like one big cocktail party, at least for people benefiting from the boom. With markets, as well as bankers' bonuses soaring, why worry?

The cocktail party analogy holds a deeper truth about why investors may have suffered from impaired decision making and poor self control during these years before the crash. This was more than a simple case of minor intuitive errors in reasoning. Instead, according to MIT finance professor Andrew Lo, the real problem is traders literally were drunk on money. As Lo testified before Congress about the origins of the credit crisis:

> "While this boom/bust pattern is familiar to macroeconomists, who have developed complex models for generating business cycles, there may be a simpler explanation based on human behavior. There is mounting evidence from cognitive neuroscientists that financial gain affects the same pleasure centers of the brain that are activated by certain narcotics. This suggests that prolonged periods of economic growth and prosperity can induce a collective sense of euphoria and complacency among investors that is not unlike the drug induced stupor of a cocaine addict...."

Lo, who is CEO of a hedge fund in addition to his work as an academic, has an interest in neuroscience. He has wired foreign exchange traders with biofeedback devices during the course of their work. When the market showed significant changes, so did the physiological response of all traders, but inexperienced traders were a lot more emotional when trading. For instance, they exhibited rising heart rates compared to the pros. For Lo, this indicates some emotion is necessary for decision making, but too much is problematic. (Neuroscience, though it has a different focus from evolutionary psychology, is consistent with and often supports the idea discussed throughout this book that humans have two decision systems—an intuitive one and an analytical one. Different responses exhibit different patterns of brain activation.)

I met with Lo at his office at MIT overlooking the Charles River. He was wearing sneakers, which made him look like either a trendy hedge fund manager or a down-to-earth academic. (Of course, he is both.) Lo explained to me how the way our brains are wired could lead to an economic crisis: "The situation had been building for 10 years. Everyone was making money all the time. Traders became confused because money was so cheap and risks were so hidden. Bond traders became caught up in a feedback loop." It is Lo's contention that the traders' brains were affected by this loop. Financial success triggered the same neural circuits as by cocaine. Said Lo: "The same neural circuitry that responds to cocaine, food, and sex has been shown to be activated by monetary gain as well."

As a result of their financial success, traders became inured to risk. In fact, they began to take on extreme financial risks—the financial equivalent of someone who is hallucinating stepping out of a 30-story building because they are certain they can fly. And to make matters worse, banks encouraged this risky behavior. Traders who refused to jump, were in effect pushed—or fired by their employers. Risk managers at large investment banks, in the months leading up to the crash, were sidelined or terminated if they warned the banks were taking on too much risk.

What this all suggests to Lo is the need for an external solution: a government intervention. If there is something hardwired in our cognitive processes that pushes us to excess, someone has got to stop us. Not everyone has the discipline to be a hyper-controlled investor and resist temptations that turn out to be damaging. Nor did financial institutions see any rationale to puncture the growing bubble. That leaves regulation as the mechanism society uses to prevent itself from indulging in self-destructive behavior.

Fire code regulation is a great example. Creating buildings with well-built emergency stairways, sprinkler systems, and clearly labeled exit signs is costly. This building infrastructure isn't free. Why not leave it up to the market to choose which buildings are fireproof and which ones are not? Those worried about fires will pay more; those less worried will choose the second type of building.

Lo explained why, as a society, we haven't left it up to the market to sort out this choice for us: "Left to our own devices, no would pay for the expensive infrastructure because when we walk into a building, our assessment of the likelihood of fire is zero," said Lo. It is a cognitive bias. Intuitively, we underestimate the probabilities of this sort of catastrophe. But as a society, we have learned the hard way that people don't worry about fires until after the fact. As a result, we put in regulation to ensure that buildings offer adequate fire safety.

The metaphor to financial markets and the crisis is clear. Here, we didn't put in regulations to prevent banks from doing what they felt comfortable with in terms of risks. There was an inadequate "financial infrastructure" in terms of strong bank regulation and adequate bank reserves in place to protect the financial system in case of a catastrophe. Banks, left to their own devices, discounted this likelihood. They pursued aggressive trading strategies that seemed safe at the time, only to create conditions that led to a collapse in prices and an eventual fire sale of assets.

Errors in judgment, therefore, aren't just ruinous to individuals: They can be damaging to society on the whole. A containable problem can quickly grow into something much worse—either a fire or a financial meltdown—if society chooses to ignore or discount people's all too predictable biases.

Lo ended our interview on a poetic note, telling me that as a society, we need to look to Odysseus for guidance: "Just as Odysseus asked his shipmates to tie him to the mast and plug his ears with wax as they sailed past the Sirens of Circe's island, we must use regulation as a tool to protect ourselves from our most self-destructive tendencies."

♦ ♦ ♦

My conversations with Rob Arnott and Andrew Lo were really about the same problem: investor irrationality. Arnott's strategy is squarely focused on improving returns, asking what is best for the investor. Lo's arguments are more macroeconomic, asking how these biased individual decisions add up collectively.

Later, I will turn to the macro issue of the role intuition played in creating the conditions that led to the financial crisis. I then explore how to build a stronger financial system, given the way humans really think and behave, including the need for better regulation. More immediately, I now turn to specific investments and how in a time of panic, rather than engaging in an irrational flight to quality, there may be more profitable ways to invest. These behaviorally based investing strategies are literally "counterintuitive." They require overcoming your own initial instincts and taking advantage of others' rush to snap judgment about investment decisions.

2

Buy High, Sell Low: The Basic Instinct Driven Error of Investing

Benjamin Graham once said, "An investor's chief problem, even his worst enemy, is likely to be himself." This is nowhere more true than when it comes to deciding to buy or sell a stock. We have an uncanny ability to buy stocks that are poor investments and sell stocks that are good investments. In essence, we buy high and sell low. In general, investors tend to shoot themselves in the foot—because they follow their instincts.

Once upon a time most economists and some investors thought people behaved rationally when it came to their money. Economic theory assumed investors, on average, would make good, even optimal decisions in terms of maximizing their wealth: Real money was at stake, so people would do the thing that earned them the most. Psychologists who study how people make decisions were under no such illusions. They knew our decisions are driven by irrational impulses, gut instincts, and the way our brains process information, rather than the cold rationality embedded in economic models. Finally, researchers stopped arguing about theory and studied how investors actually make decisions. They found that investors behave the way psychologists predicted, not the way economists predicted. Behavioral economics was born.

The most clear and startling finding came from Terry Odean, an economist at Berkeley. Odean's research is now one of the classics of the behavioral finance literature, even though arguably the field is too young to have classics. Odean studied the stock selection-decisions of individual investors. He found we do everything wrong: We trade too often for no economic gain. We are undiversified, holding only a few stocks that get our attention. The details get even more interesting. We easily sell off stocks that have done well, but we have trouble letting go of stocks that have performed badly, holding onto them in the hope they will come back. This is ruinous on two levels. By selling winners and holding onto losers, we are setting ourselves up for a tax hit, because we face taxes on stocks that have appreciated. Because stocks prices show momentum (see Chapter 12, "Momentum," for more about these effects), the stocks we have sold tend to keep rising. And the stocks we hold tend to keep falling.

Our trading patterns make no economic sense given these results, but they make a lot of psychological sense. We feel we should at least get what we paid for a stock, even if the stock market has no interest in our feelings. The behavioral economists Meir Statman and Hersh Shefrin called this the "disposition effect" as shorthand for our "pre-disposition to get-even-itis." As a result, we have trouble letting go of stocks that are worth less than we paid for them. Amplifying this impulse is the different way we experience gains and losses identified by the psychologists who pioneered behavioral economics. Losses are more painful than gains. Moreover, we are willing to gamble on the downside, to make a certain loss less certain. By holding onto our losers, we are hoping they will go up. For our stocks that are winners, we aren't compelled to gamble and want to lock in our gains. And as a result we sell our winners and hold on to our losers. Psychologically, we are satisfied, only to be punished by the stock market for our actions.

Odean was familiar with these behavioral theories and predictions. His personal history in many ways anticipated his nonconventional research agenda. Odean was a college dropout, who had worked as a New York City cab driver among other jobs, before returning to get his undergraduate degree at Berkeley at age 37. As a "mature student" he met psychologist Daniel Kahneman, the future

Nobel Laureate then in the process of refining his work on decision making. Kahneman suggested Odean continue on in graduate school in economics rather than psychology. Odean analyzed real stock-trading data for evidence of psychological factors at work, which no one had bothered to do before. He discovered how precisely trades followed the disposition effect, with investors trying to get even in terms of what they paid for a stock.

Odean remembers the reactions to his discovery at the time, way back in 1997, which is not exactly light years ago, but a very different economic environment from today. The tech bubble was just heating up. "The standard response from professors was 'Personally I think this is interesting but my colleagues won't be as open minded as I am,'" says Odean. The group dynamics at work interested him as a behaviorist. Everyone liked thinking of themselves as open minded. But at the same time, no one dared risk publicly acknowledging in a group setting the merits of the behaviorist approach.

The news media had no such hesitation. Odean's findings broke out into the press, which is rare for an economics research paper, and Odean did numerous TV appearances (though audiences were surprised to see an economist sporting an earring the size of a class ring). The profession changed its views. The disposition effect in stock trading, once a heretical idea, is now mainstream, and even arguably part of a new orthodoxy. Every financial planner warns against the human tendency to sell our winners and hold on to our losers.

This instinctive error in stock trading might still pose some dangers to investors, but has greatly diminished in impact. The effect is now widely known, and the age of the day trader is over in any case. Most trading is now done by institutional investors, where the disposition effect is less pronounced. It isn't their money, so they are less emotionally involved.

Being aware of the disposition effect is primarily a defensive strategy. (If you are trading stocks, next time you are holding on to a losing position, hoping it will come back, ask yourself how realistic this belief is. Also consider the tax consequence of selling.)

However, you can take advantage of the disposition effect exhibited by other investors. This profitable trading is one way to make money off of psychological insights about investor behavior. It is a variation on the momentum strategies discussed later in the book.

Again, central to the strategy is the fact that people don't like to sell things at a loss. This is an immensely strong behavioral bias. The way to make money is to apply this insight to earnings announcements. Suppose a company has surprisingly good earnings. The stock goes up. Investors have no trouble selling off their winners. The market becomes swamped with sellers so the price doesn't rise immediately. But let's say the opposite happens. The company has a negative earnings surprise. The stock goes down. Investors are very unlikely to realize their losses. They hold onto the stock, hoping it will come back. As a result, the price of the stock doesn't fall, at least not at first.

What this means is in both cases it takes a while for the stock price to reflect its new situation. If the stock has gone up, the dumping of shares slows down its price increase. If it goes down, the hoarding of shares slows down its price decrease. In both cases, the stock price eventually reflects its true value but takes a while to get there, giving you time to move, to buy stocks going up, and to short or sell stocks going down.

Though exploiting the disposition effect can be a profitable strategy, there is an additional factor influencing the speed of change, making returns more predictable—and that is knowing the reference point, the price at which someone purchased the stock. The disposition effect always involves a reference point. If you bought IBM at $1 and it goes up to $20 and then drops to $19, you still view it as a winner. But if it drops to 50 cents, then get-even-itis effect kicks in, quite intensely. You now are extremely reluctant to sell the stock. If there are many investors like you, the price decline will be severely slowed down. This gives hedge funds more of a profit window because the market isn't reacting instantaneously. Sophisticated hedge funds now try to identify and sort the purchase price of a stock in order to be able to identify the magnitude of the disposition effect in order to improve returns.

The trading strategy based on the disposition effect and stock price sorting was first identified by Andrea Frazzini, a finance professor at the University of Chicago Business School, who is also well known in the hedge fund world. Frazzini explains: "From my active investor point of view, I like to short stocks with bad news." But even if you aren't shorting these stocks, you should consider selling them, according to Frazzini. It won't generate enormous market-beating returns but instead may simply be the sensible thing to do. He says, "Stocks with bad earning announcements keep going down for a while. Individual investors should just sell them. Waiting can only lose you money."

For stocks with good news, waiting to sell makes sense. The disposition effect means everyone is selling, depressing the rise in price at first, but eventually it reaches fair value. Waiting eventually makes you money.

In other words, do the complete opposite of what your gut impulse tells you, as seen in the disposition effect. Sell your losers. And hold on to your winners.

3

More About Stocks: Dividends— Behavioral Ways to Play the Dividend Game

Should you buy stocks that pay a dividend? Or is better to invest in stocks that pay no dividend? Historically, most returns from investing in stocks have come from the dividend, not from appreciation in price. After the 2008 crash, the conventional wisdom is that dividend-paying stocks are the way to go, particularly when interest rates are low. But non-dividend-paying corporations might be reinvesting their earnings to pursue great growth opportunities and therefore might show better capital appreciation, meaning these stocks are the better bet. Personal finance gurus have many answers. So do behavioral economists. They find that you may think you are playing the dividend game but really you are being played by the stock-issuing corporations themselves, who are altering their dividend policy to exploit consumer beliefs about dividends.

A little background is necessary first. The question of whether dividend-paying stocks are better or worse bets has baffled economists for years. The Nobel Laureates Merton Miller and Franco Modigliani posed the question this way: "Do companies with generous distribution policies consistently sell at a premium over those with niggardly payouts? Is the reverse ever true?" They answered their own question: Theoretically it *doesn't matter* whether or not a company decides to issue a dividend. They were even able to formally prove this. Under idealized conditions, the value of a company should not be affected by whether it decides to pay out a dividend or reinvest its returns. Putting aside things such as taxes, only earnings matter. Investors shouldn't seek out dividend-paying stocks, or necessarily avoid them. In fact, the real question posed by the formal and austere models of finance is, "Why do companies issue dividends at all?"

Behavioral finance has reexamined the question of dividends and come up with an answer to the dividend question—an answer not just of interest to theoreticians, but to investors. The new approach takes into account investor beliefs and sentiments about dividends. Dividends, it turns out, do matter to share price. There are times when you should buy—or avoid—dividend-paying stocks.

Jeff Wurgler is a finance professor at NYU who studies investor sentiment and stock market value. With a colleague, Malcolm Baker of Harvard Business School, he researches situations where investors get excited about companies with certain characteristics that seem unrelated to underlying value, but can impact value anyway. Which brings us back to dividends....

As Wurgler explained to me, "Paying or not paying dividends is interpreted by investors as allowing them to categorize the firm as 'mature/safe' (one that pays dividends) or 'risky/growth' (no dividend)." That is, investors read a lot into a company's dividend policy. People believe that if a company pays a dividend, it must be somehow be less risky and more consistent in its operating results. It's a safe investment. Alternatively, investors may believe that if a company had great growth opportunities, it wouldn't waste money paying out a dividend. So a dividend is a sign of a low growth, whereas not paying a dividend implies the company has big potential, although there are no guarantees.

The popularity of dividend-paying stocks comes in waves. At times investors love them, and at times investors hate them. During 1950s, it was common for rich investors to live on their dividends. And today, many retirees continue with this more traditional view of investing, never buying or selling a stock but instead seeking out dividend-paying stocks for income. During the tech boom, dividends were a sign to investors that a company was old economy. Nothing was more passé than a dividend; it indicated a company had run out of growth ideas. Only a few years later, investors interpreted a stock being able to pay a dividend as a sign of strength, and a good bet. Microsoft's decision to start issuing dividends in 2003 was the watershed between these two recent eras.

This market sentiment about dividends, whether they are hot or not, shows up in stock prices.

Investors start paying a premium for stocks with dividends when they are in favor, and discount them when they are out of favor. Wurgler and Baker's research shows that since the 1960s investors have gone through four or five cycles of paying premiums or discounts for stocks that pay dividends. Dividends do matter to a stock's value, depending on whether or not they are in fashion.

Corporations aren't passive onlookers to these trends. Wurgler (who consults for a money manager) explains that companies are aware of when there is a premium on paying dividends, and when there is a discount. Executives get a sense of what the market wants— they see a competitor with the same product line but who pays a dividend get a better valuation. Or their investment banker stops by and tells them to add a dividend. And, of course, they have to listen to comments at the annual meeting and get a sense of what's in the air.

And so they respond. They play the dividend game, "switching teams" if necessary, either becoming dividend payers when the market is hot or stopping when it's not. It's just like during the dot com era when companies quickly added ".com" to their names, and after the bubble, in the same way, they found it convenient to drop the ".com." Only this time the focus is on dividends. Wurgler phrases it this way: "If the market wants pizza, you deliver pizza. If it rewards dividends, then you start issuing them."

This pizza analogy (Wurgler and Baker formally term it a catering theory, because companies "cater" to investor demands for dividends) captures a lot of recent corporate moves regarding dividends. In fact, Wurgler's theory precisely describes the reasons companies themselves have given as to why they decide to start paying dividends. For instance, take Microsoft's momentous move to start issuing a dividend in 2003.

Market commentary at the time focused on Microsoft's decision as a sign—that the company was finally growing up, but also that it was running out of places to invest its cash. Here are some sample insights from stock analysts: "Paying a dividend speaks to the end of the growth and the beginning of maturity" (Bob Austrian, Banc of America Securities). "They have an extreme amount of cash that's dragging down the return on equity" (Robert Schwartz, Thomas Weisel Partners). "I think [Microsoft] is sending a message to shareholders that the story has changed from one of a high-growth company to a mature company" (Scott McAdams, McAdams Wright Ragen).

Contrast these with Microsoft's own comments about why they started issuing a dividend: "We believe...an annual dividend will make Microsoft stock even more attractive to a broader range of investors," according to the company's CFO, John Connors. Microsoft spokeswoman Caroline Boren added that increasing the field of investors "was most certainly part of the thinking behind the decision." In another words, the reason the company issued a dividend was because investors wanted one. And it wasn't much of a dividend: The payout was only 0.3% of Microsoft's share price. Microsoft's CFO characterized it as a "starter dividend."

This new behavioral approach to dividends is a cynical one, even a nihilistic one. There are few fixed truths about the decision to start issuing dividends, only changing investment fashions. Instead of reading dividends as holding some deep meaning about a company's prospects, the company might instead just be reading what's on your mind. (The behavioral theory applies to a company's decision to start issuing a dividend, not the size of the payout, which is usually related to profitability.)

But investors can play the behavioral dividend game, too. Managers who issue dividends to exploit market sentiment are playing one side, but you can play the other. The central insight from the new behavioral research on dividends is that firms that issue them get overvalued when dividends are hot, and undervalued when they aren't. Therefore, investors can "lean into the wind" and take a contrarian approach, investing in passé non-dividend-paying stocks when dividends are in fashion and maybe shorting the dividend payers. The idea is that eventually firms that are overvalued because they are paying dividends will eventually return to fair value.

This contrarian approach takes time. Investors have to wait for stocks to revert to the mean. Wurgler warns not to bet the farm. The bigger question for investors is: How do we know if we are in a period when dividend-paying firms are overvalued or undervalued? We don't have investment bankers dropping by to tell us. Here is Wurgler's suggestion: "Ask the least informed but most confident person you know who has a strong opinion about dividend-paying stocks—and then do the opposite."

4

Bonds: Malign Neglect

At a cocktail party in Litchfield County, Connecticut, several summers ago, money was the subtext of almost every conversation. Litchfield County, for those who don't know it, is a rural area of northwestern Connecticut favored by Wall Streeters and other New Yorkers who find the Hamptons to be too much of a scene. The aspirations are slightly different as well, tending toward colonial New England and vague hints of a WASP pedigree supported by displays of collections of early American furniture. Guests at the party talked of many things, such as the impact of the new green resort coming to town, or what they thought of the President. The real-estate agent, the best source of gossip, held forth on who was divorcing and who was trading up in their spouse and house. But most conversations tended to circle back to wealth and investing—how much the neighbors had, who had made a killing in real estate, and who had the biggest hedge fund. But there was one investment, one asset class, no one talked about: bonds.

This cocktail party is not a hypothetical example—I was there. I was the host. Despite the small sample size of just a few people at a party, I think we can generalize: People don't brag about their bonds at cocktail parties, or ever. I have never, ever heard a "hot" bond tip. At best, we view them as an "also ran" of an asset class. But we ignore bonds at our peril.

After the credit crunch and the dramatic fall of the stock market, many of my Litchfield, Connecticut, guests looked at bonds completely differently. It is likely they wished they had invested more heavily in government bonds. Treasuries were one of the few safe harbors during the credit crunch. But what is equally likely is their portfolios were devastated by their high-yield bonds. High-yield bonds are non-investment-grade bonds. Their former name was "junk," but they have been successfully rebranded to keep the focus on their higher returns rather than higher risks. When all bonds looked alike, and almost all returns were low, why not just invest in a high yield? The answer became clear during the blowout of high yield in the Fall of '08 when their old name of "junk" seemed more apt.

We ignore bonds for largely psychological reasons. Bonds are complicated. The bond market is opaque; credit risk is complex; commissions on bond trades are hard to figure out. At a more basic level, many features of bonds are not intuitive, including the most basic: the inverse relationship between interest rates and price. A survey of wealthy bond owners conducted by *The Wall Street Journal* astonishingly found that only a fraction were aware that when interest rates go up, bond prices fall. When interest rates go down, the price of bonds rises. (For those who got it wrong in the poll, here is why the relationship is inverse: Let's say you are holding a bond that pays a specific amount. Interest rates rise, and new bonds out there now yield more than yours. If you want to sell your bond, you have to offer something comparable to a buyer. The only way to do that is to lower the price, so that when the bond eventually matures, the buyer gets that much more than he paid for it. Or here is an even simpler way of looking at it: Your bond offers a certain yield. Interest rates go up and newly issued bonds have higher yields. No one wants to buy yours now, and the price drops as a result).

Even financial planners specializing in bonds get confused: A survey of advisors by AllianceBernstein, the investment management firm, found only 38% believed they understood fixed-income markets "very well or well." A follow-up question, asked of a different set of advisors, revealed that even these low numbers were too high. A mere 27% were able to correctly define "bond duration." Though "duration" sounds like it has something to do with length of time, bond duration is actually a measure of sensitivity to interest rates.

But most fundamentally, bonds are boring. They aren't sexy. They don't usually have a huge upside, the way stocks do. And before the credit crunch the media never talked about them, only stocks. This lack of understanding, combined with lack of excitement, creates certain behavioral pathologies when it comes to bond investing.

One error is even when we make an appropriate allocation to bonds, we aren't diversified enough *within* the portfolio of bonds we own. Personal finance gurus repeat the message to diversify, diversify, diversify over and over, but they almost always are talking about the overall asset allocation or among stocks, never among bonds. If anything, diversification is more urgent in fixed income than in equities, because bonds, unlike stocks, march together. Investors may be unaware that diversifying into different issues and types of bonds—such as munis (municipal bonds), corporate bonds, or even emerging-market bonds—has the potential to decrease their risks and increase their returns.

Here individuals run into a problem with the bond market—a real one, not one in their heads. Diversifying your bond portfolio is almost impossible to do by yourself. Individual bonds are too expensive and hard to trade to be able to create a diversified portfolio unless you are extremely wealthy. And even if you have the financial resources, the work required to figure out the right price for a bond, to say nothing of attempting credit analysis on your own, is immense. Take, for instance, Lehman Brothers, which received an "A" credit rating (but should have been rated XXX) five days before going broke. Understanding Lehman's true credit risk was beyond most individual and institutional investors, including apparently Lehman itself. To avoid Lehman-type disasters, the solution again is to diversify. The easiest and most efficient way to do this is through a mutual fund or multisector bond fund that can spread the risk across the bond market, and undertake the credit analysis for you.

Munis

Individuals can easily invest in municipal bonds, known as "munis," on their own, without using a fund. Historically, 70% of munis have been held by individuals rather than institutions. Munis offer tax advantages and therefore make a lot of sense for those who have to pay high income taxes. According to old bond hands, when buying munis, it is possible to diversify *within* the muni sector because, at least in states like California, there is a large traded market, offering lots of credit diversification. This theory ran into trouble when the muni sector was hit hard by the credit crunch.

Individual investors have a strange kink when it comes to municipal bonds. We tend to buy munis that trade at par, which is bond-speak for face value. For instance, let's suppose a bond has a face value of $1,000 and is also trading at $1,000, while offering an interest rate of 5%. It is therefore trading at "par." But the price of the bond can fluctuate, depending on interest rates. If interest rates go up to say, 6%, demand for the $1,000 bond will fall and its price will drop. Or if interest rates fall, demand for the bond will rise, and prices will rise. The larger point is that buying bonds at par offers no real advantage, except some sort of psychological advantages.

"Investors like the simplicity of round numbers," observes Eric Jacobson, director of Fixed Income Strategies at Morningstar, "and they like buying bonds at par; they avoid buying at a premium or a discount over the par price." Buying bonds at par makes the investment easier to keep track of because the starting point is clearer. But it also makes the investors easier to pick off by professional bond traders and salesman. The industry is well aware of individual investors' proclivity to buy muni bonds at par. In the same way that fisherman cluster during the night at lit piers that attract fish strangely drawn to light, industry insiders compete to exploit small investors' love of par bonds—they are rich fishing grounds for the industry.

There is an old industry axiom that when a manager has a bond he doesn't like, he sells into retail. Says Jacobson, "It is well known that individuals like par bonds. The big national brokers offer par muni bonds to little regional brokers, who will look for a client who wants the bond." But what is wrong with many of these bonds is that they are callable. A callable bond is one where the issuer has the right to redeem the bond earlier than its maturity date. They can be extremely volatile, depending on which way interest rates go, even if they are selling at par. The industry term for this volatility is cuspy— they are at the cusp of being called. Says Jacobson, "The individual is sold a bond at par that looks stable and simple but in fact is extremely cuspy and volatile, the sort of bond you don't want in your portfolio." The solution for individuals is recognizing their hang-ups about par bonds and not being in any rush to buy them.

Decisions

The credit crunch, if nothing else, should have changed our perceptions that bonds are boring. It also exposed the failures of most professional bond managers. As bonds yielded less and less, they increased their gambles more and more, not realizing bonds were about to fall off a cliff. At the same time, bonds remain mostly a game for professionals; the industry wasn't set up for individual investors, and most traders seem happy to keep it that way.

This creates a dilemma for investors. You can invest in government bonds or a bond index on your own with no outside help, but otherwise using a bond mutual fund or professional bond manager is the easiest way to go. Even as a savvy investor, you don't have the portfolio size or access to information and credit analysis to properly price bonds. And, if you did, the pricing still works against you because fixed income is an institutional market that occasionally lets individuals in, only to scalp them the most. All these factors favor using a professional or mutual fund for your bond investing. But given the recent shortcomings and outright failures of even the most famous names in fixed income, do you trust the professionals and want to give them your money again? That's psychologically a tough one. I don't have a good answer for you.

5

The Psychology of Why People (Used to) Hate Annuities

Take the following retirement quiz about two people who have made permanent decisions on how to spend a portion of their money in retirement. Which sounds like a better deal to you?

Quiz #1

Each person has some savings and can spend $1,000 each month from Social Security in addition to the portion of income mentioned in each question. They have already set aside money to leave for their children when they die. The choices are intended to be financially equivalent and based on personal preferences for spending in retirement.

Mr. Red: Mr. Red can spend $650 each month for as long as he lives in addition to Social Security. When he dies, there will be no more payments.

Mr. Gray: Mr. Gray can choose an amount to spend each month in addition to Social Security. How long his money lasts depends on how much he spends. If he spends only $400 per month, he has money for as long as he lives. When he dies, he may leave the remainder to charity. If he spends $650 per month, he has money only until age 85. He can spend down faster or slower than each of these options.

Results: How did you answer? It is likely that you felt Mr. Red had a better deal than Mr. Gray. His consumption was guaranteed for life whereas Mr. Gray risked running out of money after age 85.

This financial quiz (actually a psychological experiment) was developed by the economists Jeffrey Brown, Jeffrey Kling, Sendhil Mullainathan, and Marian V. Wrobel, who wanted to understand what factors went into people's retirement decisions. They found the majority of participants when presented with this exact choice preferred Mr. Red's situation to Mr. Gray's.

Then the economists varied the experiment slightly. They rewrote the setup paragraph using new language and new descriptions, which conveyed a slightly different message. They tested it on a new group of participants.

Here is their new quiz. Try taking it. You might not change your answer because you have already seen the original version. Nonetheless, try reading the introductory paragraphs slowly and carefully, letting it put you in a new frame of mind before making your decision.

Quiz #2

Two people have made permanent decisions on how to spend a portion of their money in retirement. Which sounds like a better deal to you?

Each person has some savings and receives $1,000 each month in social security, in addition to the portion of savings mentioned in each question. Each person has chosen a different way to invest this portion ($100,000) of their savings. They have already set aside money to leave for their children when they die. The choices are intended to be financially equivalent and based on personal preferences for investing in retirement.

Mr. Red: Mr. Red invests $100,000 in an account which earns $650 each month for as long as he lives. He can only withdraw the earnings he receives, not the invested money. When he dies, the earnings will stop and his investment will be worth nothing.

Mr. Gray: Mr. Gray invests $100,000 in an account which earns a 4% interest rate. He can withdraw some or all of the invested money at any time. When he dies, he may leave any remaining money to charity.

Results: The majority of people who took *this* quiz said Mr. Gray had a better deal.

Quiz #1 and Quiz #2 are, of course, exactly the same in financial terms. But in psychological terms they couldn't be more different, because of the differences in language and descriptions. In the first quiz, everything is presented in terms of consumption: Mr. Red and Mr. Gray *spend* the money. When taking the quiz, you are confronted with the consumption consequences of financial decision. The second quiz emphasizes investments. It uses words such as invest and earnings. It mentions the account balance. When taking this quiz, you think about the return on the investment.

Psychologically, these differences in perspectives are known as frames. The underlying information is the same, but we filter it and make our decisions depending on how the choices are couched. When the financial decision is framed as a consumption decision, Mr. Red's guaranteed spending money looks the good deal. When the financial decision is framed as an investment decision, Mr. Gray's opportunity to invest his money looks like a better deal. In another words, context can be as important as content when it comes to financial decisions, even very important financial decisions.

I spoke to Mr. Brown (this is beginning to sound like a Quentin Tarantino gangster movie where each character is named after a different color, but here I am referring to the eminent economist Jeffrey Brown of the University of Illinois who cocreated this experiment). He said this of his results: "Traditionally, economists have had the underlying view that people are hyper-rational and are trying to maximize their happiness (what economists call utility). If you believe that, then how you package the information shouldn't impact their decisions. But you have huge swings in how people behave depending on how the information is packaged."

The larger point of the experiment is not just that framing has an impact; it is specifically about how retirement planning is "framed" in the U.S. and how we are conditioned to think about it. Should our financial focus be on building wealth for retirement, or on what we can consume after we retire? Is the right measure of financial success how much wealth we have when we retire? Or how much we can spend each month after we retire? Like the quiz, these are different ways of looking at essentially the same problem.

It is Jeffrey Brown's contention that we have been conditioned to think about retirement as mostly an investment decision, similar to quiz #2. Whereas he feels thinking about retirement as largely a consumption decision, similar to quiz #1, is more appropriate. Says Brown, "The messages that individuals receive when encouraged to save are all about how much you have in your account and your rates of return. But really you should think about how much can you eat each month, how much can you consume." This subtle conditioning or "framing" has a real result when we retire. Most people see themselves as Mr. Gray and choose the investment solution. However, most economists feel we should be in a consumption frame of mind, and follow Mr. Red's choice.

If it is not already clear, Mr. Red has bought an annuity: $650 a month. The experiment is an attempt to explain why annuities are so unpopular, despite their many economic advantages.

Annuities

There are rational reasons to buy an annuity when you retire. The foremost is you don't have to worry about outliving your money. With a guaranteed check coming in each month, you need never live your final years in poverty. On top of this, annuities also have the potential for higher returns than from traditional investments because of their inbuilt insurance features—if you survive that is. For people who make it into their 90s, the income from an investment in traditional assets would only be 40% compared to the income from the same amount of money spent on an annuity. The fact that people aren't necessarily good at handling their money once they have retired makes the arguments in favor of annuities even more compelling. This is why the wildly enthusiastic consensus among most economists, to say nothing of the insurance industry, is that annuities are a great thing.

But the consensus among the public is that annuities aren't so hot: Only a tiny fraction of people buy them. Many people hate annuities, which puzzles academics. Hence, economist Franco Modigliani, in his Nobel Prize acceptance speech, said, "It is a well-known fact that (individual) annuity contracts...are extremely rare. Why this should be so is a subject of considerable current interest. It is still ill understood."

It is no longer so "ill understood." The answer has to do with human psychology. Annuities, until recently, were a bad match for what most people, as opposed to most economists, worried about. One rational reason not to buy annuities is they tend to be very expensive, with the pricing opaque and hard to figure out. Also, they make the most sense if you plan to live a long time, and therefore attract people who are unusually good at doing this. Insurance companies have noticed, and priced annuities accordingly, meaning they are costly. They aren't actuarially fair, and the pricing favors the long lived instead of the general population. And they have some risks: Because they are contracts with individual corporations, if the insurer goes bust, there goes your annuity. Finally, annuities are complex and hard to understand, and people don't like complexity. The complexity starts with the name, with many things called an "annuity" that aren't annuitized. For instance, insurance companies offer products with annuity in their name that really resemble mutual funds: You don't have to surrender your principal and they don't guarantee lifetime income. The annuities I am referring to are "life annuities"—irrevocable insurance products that in exchange for a payment offer a minimum level of guaranteed income that lasts a lifetime.

The central problem is framing: Consumers view annuities as risky gambles rather than insurance. If we die early, we lose; if we live a long time, we win. Economists, and insurance companies, view annuities as insurance: not against dying but against the risk of *outliving* your wealth. They call this longevity risk—the risk that you live longer than you expected and have budgeted for. Anyone else would consider living to a ripe old age a good thing. Not economists who fret about all the financial dangers involved, which can be mostly taken care of by annuities.

This brings us back to Jeffrey Brown's framing experiment. Says Brown, "If I think about how much money I have in a bank, then an annuity looks horrible. I am giving up a lump of wealth and whether I get it back or not depends on how long I live; so it seems risky. But if I think about how much I am going to be able to spend every day, then an annuity looks great."

Insurance companies are well aware of our psychological problems with annuities, and current behavioral economics research into this area. Their psychological insights are allowing them to engineer products that meet consumer's psychological as well as financial needs. This includes "reframing" our perception of annuities by highlighting their insurance features. Some annuities are now explicitly offered as longevity "insurance"—these are usually ones designed to kick in very late in life, at 85 plus. Or another idea is to link an annuity to long-term care insurance, a sort of two-for-one product, addressing two big concerns of the elderly: cash flow and healthcare. Variable annuities try to emphasize growth and income, appealing to our desire for both. The biggest changes are in "guaranteed death benefits." Insurance companies are trying to take the "gambling with your life" feature out of annuities, through guaranteed death benefits. The idea is you, or rather your estate and beneficiaries, get the money back if you die before the annuity has kicked in. In fact, the development of annuity products is so rapid and extensive, much of it based on applications of behavioral economics, that insurance companies, once seen as plodding and dull, are at the center of financial innovation. It looks like they will succeed in making annuities popular.

But I still see challenges ahead because there is one remaining big psychological—and real—problem with annuities, and that is control. If you buy an annuity, you give up control of your money. Maybe the insurer will let you buy the annuity back, but such a rider is extremely expensive. And a true annuity is irrevocable. "Irrevocable" is not an easy concept or word to swallow. Once you buy an annuity, the money is no longer yours. Before you had, say $1,000,000. After the purchase, it now is the insurance company's. You get a check every month, but you no longer have the $1,000,000 to play with.

Even though an annuity reduces the risk you won't outlive your money, there are other risks to worry about, like the risk you won't have enough money exactly when you need it, if you get really sick, for instance, or have a sick grandchild. It doesn't have to be so morbid: You might prefer the flexibility of playing with your money. For all I know, you might have the desire to buy a $15,000 bottle of champagne and spray it around a nightclub, or go on a mega shopping trip to Dubai and end up broke afterward. These might be your desires. But it would be hard to live your dream on your carefully doled out "oldster" allowance in the form of an annuity from your insurance company.

So the question comes down to this: Do you want all your consumption needs insured in the form of annuity, or just some or maybe none of them? I don't think this is about being rational versus irrational; it's just a matter of your tastes, how you want to invest your money, and how you want to spend it.

6

The Psychology of Selecting Mutual Funds

How do we pick a particular mutual fund to invest in? The answer is very simple: Its performance last year, last quarter, or even last month. Of course, advertising helps, too, but "returns-chasing behavior" as it is technically known, pretty much captures our actions when it comes to mutual fund choices. The #1 fund in the country last year in terms of performance will be near or at the top of mutual funds attracting the most new investment dollars.

And performance here means absolute raw performance, not adjusted for risks, fees, taxes, or compared to a benchmark such as the S&P 500. If it makes more money than we paid for it, we see it as a winner, even if the S&P did much better. Alternatively, if a mutual fund is below what we paid for it, but every other investment is doing significantly worse, we aren't impressed.

But after we make our performance-related investment choice, our one moment of action, we as investors appear to go to sleep. Our inbuilt inertia and apparent passivity when it comes to investing take over. We open an account and then sit on our hands. The fund may stumble, but we don't seem to react. We leave our investment where it is. Most investors don't reallocate from low-performing to high-performing funds, even within their portfolio. Returns-chasing behavior, therefore, only goes in one direction: We give new assets to high-performing funds, but leave old assets with the underperforming managers. An unattractive analogy is to roach motels: We check in, but don't check out.

This returns-chasing behavior is seemingly hardwired in humans, from the most naive individual investors to the most sophisticated institutional investors. Everyone does it. It is why hedge funds, which may have had their highest returns in the 1980s and 1990s (although no one knows for sure), became such a popular investment a decade later, even though their best days were probably long behind them as a strategy. Financial planners, in surveys, *say* they don't chase returns, but an analysis of their investment choices by Daniel Bergstresser of Harvard Business School found plenty of evidence of it. And we know that returns chasing is what drives individual investors in their choice of mutual funds.

Returns chasing isn't automatically a bad strategy. In most circumstances, learning about the track record and history of what you are investing in should be valuable information. Even so, as every investment prospectus warns us, in a rare moment of clarity, "past returns are no guarantee of future returns." This is true, but do past returns tell us *anything* about future returns when it comes to mutual funds? They do, but not in ways we might assume.

Performance and Persistence

Alpha is the catchphrase bandied about by hedge fund managers and other finance types as shorthand for their market-beating performance (in another words, their skill). Sometimes called "Jensen's alpha," it is a technical measure of the "excess return" on an investment compared to what the market would give you, adjusted for risk. For hedge funds, alpha is their mantra, their obsession, maybe even their mojo. It's everywhere in their speeches and publications and the names of their conferences. They call each other "alpha" males. Mutual funds managers keep a bit quieter about alpha, but nonetheless mention it, too.

The word alpha, as used in a financial context, was coined in the 1960s by Michael Jensen, then a graduate student at the University of

Chicago. He was interested in mutual fund performance—was it based on a manager's skill from picking stocks or just the market going up or down on its own? He had to figure out a way to measure this, which is when he invented the concept of "alpha." He defined this as "a risk-adjusted measure of portfolio performance that estimates how much a manager's forecasting ability contributes to the fund's returns." Alpha was indeed an analytical breakthrough—the word and concept stuck and is now part of financial culture.

But that is only part one of Jensen's story. There is a second part that is completely forgotten, at least by hedge fund guys. And that is what happened when Jensen went looking for evidence of alpha in his study. He couldn't find any, at least over an extended period of time. The mutual funds he studied were not able to beat the market for any long time period. Examining the performance of mutual funds for the period 1945 to 1964, Jensen concludes: "The evidence on mutual fund performance indicates that these 115 mutual funds were not on average able to predict security prices well enough to outperform a buy-the-market-and-hold policy. Also there is very little evidence that any individual fund was able to do significantly better than that which we expected from mere random chance.... On average the funds apparently were not quite successful enough in their trading activities to recoup even their brokerage expenses."

The ability to beat the market for a specified period is known, at least by academics, as persistence. Though Jensen didn't use the word persistence when writing about alpha, it is implicit in his measure and another of his discoveries. As he modestly wrote to me when I asked him about this research: "I do not recall the idea of persistence being in existence before my study, but the study was a long time ago."

Everyone still talks about alpha, but no one talks about persist-ence. An investment manager might get lucky once or twice, but whether he or she can *persist* in generating excess returns over the market for more than a few months is really the question—and the question you should ask when selecting a fund that claims to be able to beat the market. If you ever meet a fund manager who brags about his alpha, you can ask it of him directly: "What about your persistence. How long can you keep it up?" (There might be a less aggressive way of asking this, but the point remains).

If mutual funds can't persist in beating the market, then returns chasing makes no sense as a strategy. Doing better than the market in the past is no guide to the future. The question of persistence in mutual fund performance is an unsettled one. It has been studied extensively since Jensen's day. Most academics are intrinsically skeptical that a mutual fund would be able to beat the market for very long. They use seemingly noncommittal but in fact savage language, claiming that any real evidence of persistence of market outperformance by mutual fund managers is "elusive."

Wall Street has a different view, of course. There is always the example of Peter Lynch, who ran Fidelity's Magellan Fund and had returns almost double the S&P for many years. Part of the discussion of persistence has to do with the time period you are talking about. There are managers such as Bill Miller of Legg Mason who had great runs for a while. Miller had a 15-year winning streak, only to be followed by a 10-year losing streak. This culminated in his disastrous 2008 presentation at an investment conference in New York. The topic: "The Credit Cycle—What's Next?" Miller recommended financial stocks as a great buy. He singled out Bear Stearns, in which he was one of the biggest investors, having committed $200 million of his fund's money. An audience member raised his hand and asked Miller a question: Was he aware that Bear Stearns was in crisis, in fact was cratering that *very morning*? Miller seemed shaken. He quickly left the conference. His $200-million dollar investment was soon worth only $15 million dollars.

Miller's downfall is exceptional, but it is also clear that many mutual fund managers have exceptional skills at picking stocks, as Miller himself did for a while. Mutual funds have some great years, extraordinary years, that can't be explained by dumb luck. So, what's really going on here in terms of persistence and performance?

How Our Behavior Damages Our Investments

"If someone was the top performing guy last year, is he going to be the star this year? The answer is no, no matter how much you torture the data." This question, and answer, was posed to me by Andrea Frazzini of the University of Chicago and AQR Capital. His research is very empirical, almost forensic, in indentifying patterns in financial markets, including mutual fund persistence and also trend chasing. His story about mutual funds is very simple. We, as investors, chase performance, but in doing so damage the performance of the very funds we are chasing. We are killing the thing we love.

Frazzini interprets trend chasing this way: "Your brain sees trends and patterns. In the jungle you see a shadow and you jump out of the shadow. In finance, you see a mutual fund manager who had a good return last year and so the money flows in." This story, so far, is consistent with our intuitive tendency to extrapolate past trends that underlies so much of our financial behavior and also our financial mistakes. But why doesn't the winning trend continue?

The answer is what the fund has to do in response to all the new investment money flowing in: It has to go out and buy more of the underlying stocks. For example, in 1999, people liked tech stocks in general and Cisco in particular. Huge amounts of money flowed into tech mutual funds holding Cisco. Janus funds alone, which were heavily invested in tech stocks, had inflows of $37 billion dollars, much more so than the much larger Fidelity funds, which had few tech stocks.

The more money that went to Janus, the more Cisco it had to buy. It eventually drove up the price of Cisco to unsustainable levels. The price of Cisco then fell. On top of this, all the new inflows drove up trading costs for the mutual funds. Basically the mutual funds got swamped and overwhelmed by all of the new investors. "By return chasing, people were influencing the underlying stock prices, which then had lower future returns, destroying the trend," says Frazzini. "Reallocations caused wealth destruction to mutual fund investors as Janus and tech stocks performed horribly after 1999."

Actually, the story gets worse from there. As we know, investors chase performance only one way. They tend not to withdraw their money from underperforming funds, and mutual funds can persist in underperformance. The money tends to stick, even though tech mutual funds went through *years* of terrible performance following the bubble. When people eventually sold, if at all, it was too late. In essence, for mutual funds, "people buy high and sell low," says Frazzini, which is of course the opposite of what you should be doing.

So what should you be doing? For most investors, the best advice is, instead of trend chasing, to look for funds with broad allocations that aren't concentrated in the hot sector of the moment, and that have no or low loads, low turnover, low fees, and low expenses. Staying put, unless the fund is continuously underperforming its benchmark, makes sense, too. "My opinion is turning over mutual funds a lot is not a good idea," says Frazzini. "Individuals have a striking ability to do the wrong thing. They send their money to mutual funds which own stocks that do poorly over the subsequent few years."

But there is a more sophisticated idea that arises from Frazzini's research. And that is to make a short-term momentum play with mutual funds, constantly buying and then selling outperformers, holding them for a relatively short window of time. The insight is based on Frazzini's research that a mutual fund can persist in outperforming the market and its peers for about three months. During this period, returns chasing behavior drives up prices even higher. Thereafter, the fund gets swamped and poor returns set in.

Though returns chasing is generally a bad idea for investing, your knowledge of other investors' predictable behavior can, in this case, make it work for you. Therefore, look at mutual funds' *very recent* track records, identify the hottest fund, and invest in advance of the herd of returns chasers. But make sure you have sight of the exit because you will be leaving the fund in only three months. Though it looks like you are joining those in the herd, you are really just riding them.

7

Building Your Portfolio the Behavioral Economics Way

"My image of how people form portfolios is they walk down the aisles of the financial supermarket, picking up some cereal (buying one company's stock), sardines (buying another stock), adding in some cheese or whatever tempts them, and once the cart is full proceed to check out. That becomes their portfolio." Meir Statman, a finance Professor at Santa Clara University, offers this harsh view of portfolio construction and securities selection. An early proponent of behavioral finance, Statman strongly believes we choose investments during a mindless walk, though not a random one, with little reflection about how everything fits together in our overall portfolio.

Ample empirical evidence shows that people don't think holistically about the impact on their portfolio when making investment decisions. For instance, one study of the 401(k) accounts of employees of a large U.S. retail chain found employees allocated 46% of their portfolio to company stock. This is not a wise investment allocation and an intensely risky proportion. One reason why this number was sky high was the way the 401(k) was structured. The company matched any contributions to the retirement plan with its own stock. Employees on their own chose a 23% allocation, and the company match effectively doubled this.

However, the employer changed its 401(k) policy, no longer automatically matching with company stock. It was now up to the employee to decide the components of the match. The employees

now made better portfolio decision. They allocated 23% of their portfolio in *total* to company stock.

Yale economist James Choi and several colleagues have studied
this 401(k) plan in detail for evidence of how people make portfolio
decisions. Explains Choi, "Before they didn't think about what their
employer was doing. After the change, the employees were forced to
integrate both accounts in their heads." Under the original plan, the
match in company stock was not salient or obvious to employees.
They didn't think about it when making their allocations, or didn't
seem to notice. But Choi argues that once the employees were forced
to decide what went into the match, the match got their full attention.
They made better decisions, reducing their exposure to company
stock.

Behavioral economists call this lack of integration "mental
accounting." It means making decisions for an individual account
without thinking about other accounts or the portfolio on the whole.
We appear to naturally create separate psychological accounts in our
heads when thinking about our wealth. We have mental budgets: play
money, transportation money, retirement money. Mental accounting
comes into play for income, too. Money you have saved through hard
work is treated very differently from an unexpected windfall: You are
more likely to immediately go out and spend a surprise check compared to your regular paycheck.

Mental accounting, in the case of choosing investments without
thinking about the overall portfolio, can be a problem. But on the
other hand it is a way to stay on budget and control spending; it saves
time and mental energy. The real problem is though we all do mental
accounting, neither portfolio theory nor financial planning practice
has fully acknowledged it.

Modern Portfolio Theory

The basic theoretical concept involved in building a portfolio is very old: Don't put all your eggs in one basket. But this was formalized only after World War II, by Harry Markowitz. Markowitz won a Nobel Prize for his efforts, in what he called "modern portfolio theory." This was essentially a mathematical proof that showed the way to build portfolios that had the highest return for the least risk. One idea is that diversification isn't based on how *many* stocks you own; it is whether the stocks' prices move together or separately. Uncorrelated assets provide greater diversification.

Modern portfolio theory, as developed by Markowitz, was a huge advance for economics and finance. Much that came after it was built on his mathematical insights. However, it is not that easy to implement Markowitz's ideas pragmatically. Financial planning software used today is based on Markowitz's findings, and it attempts to find the optimal portfolio by plugging in technical measures such as variance and covariance. The entire process hinges on the investor's risk tolerance, a very elusive concept (discussed in the next chapter). Aside from this last measure, Markowitz's theories are largely mathematical, with little apparent room for mental accounting.

Postmodern Portfolio Theory

"There is the rational theory of how you should behave, and how people do behave. This distinguishes traditional economics from behavioral economics." This insight was provided to me by Harry Markowitz himself. Though you would think Markowitz would, by definition, be old school, falling into the rationalist camp, this isn't true at all. In fact, Markowitz, the father of modern portfolio theory, could also be termed the "grandfather of behavioral economics." His insights, years before behavioral finance was developed, included recognizing that we react to gains and losses asymmetrically. If you have a sudden windfall, you are more likely to take, in his words, a "devil may care" attitude toward it.

Now in his 80s, Markowitz's current project is combining the traditional approach to portfolio optimization, which he invented, and mental accounting, which comes from behavioral finance. It incorporates behavioral concepts of how we think about portfolios, as developed by Hersh Shefrin and Meir Statman. Statman is his coauthor on the new work. Although the project sounds contradictory at face value, Markowitz assured me this isn't the case.

"My work always assumed you wanted an efficient combination of risk and return, the minimum risk for a given level of return. That was the maxim. To be inefficient means to be able to increase your reward without increasing risk," said Markowitz. "But investors don't think about efficient frontiers, they think in mental accounts, sub portfolios, or buckets that have their own objectives. One bucket is to prevent you from becoming a bag lady. Another bucket is to make you wealthy. A bucket in between is your bread and butter."

The project is to figure out a way to be able to think in mental accounting terms, and still create an overall portfolio that is "efficient." Markowitz and Statman claim this is theoretically possible. You just run different portfolios for each objective. The advantage, if this works, is that instead of having one portfolio that might meet all your needs, you can actually have several that meet each of them precisely, with an appropriate level of risk and return: a retirement fund, a college education fund, a rainy day fund, a travel fund. This corresponds to the way people keep mental accounts. To avoid the risk of becoming a bag lady, you would want to be heavily in treasuries, so you are never on the street. The "get rich quick account," which you aren't really counting on to work out, would include hedge funds and maybe even what's left of mortgage-backed securities.

These insights might not be so revolutionary to investors, but they are to financial planners. In fact, they may someday transform financial planning as much as Markowitz's earlier math proofs did.

The planners will create multiple portfolios for each client to meet different needs, with an appropriate asset mix and level of risk for each objective. By structuring portfolios in people's natural language, clients can have "efficient" portfolios and still feel comfortable. If equities are down 40%, the client will be reminded that is why they also had a safety portfolio of low-yielding bonds. It was there just in case.

An even simpler way to do this is to take your basic portfolio and psychologically "frame" different pieces, earmarking them for different purposes. The risky portion might be thought of as a potential legacy for the kids, the safe portion can represent your basic food and shelter needs. This can work for husbands and wives who have a joint portfolio but different ideas about money. If the husband is mostly concerned about retirement and the wife about getting rich, the financial advisor can psychologically *label* the safe part of the investment spectrum, consisting mostly of bonds, as the husband's portfolio, and the risky portion as the wife's.

For people who want it straight, and don't want things "reframed" to meet their psychological propensities, or even kinks, what portfolio advice does Markowitz have? "Turn off your TV and never watch a finance show. Or rather turn it to the food channel." His point is to stick to your stocks and bonds and don't trade too much, just buy and hold. But his larger point, and the central implication of his research is to diversify. "I don't have a daily TV show, but if I did I would get on every day and say 'diversify.' That would be the whole show. The next day I would be on again and they would say, 'What is your financial advice today, Mr. Markowitz?' and I would say 'diversify.'"

8

Risk Tolerance and Investing

In 2004, Robert Young Pelton was hiking in the dreaded Darien Gap, a remote and wild area of the Colombian jungle that straddles the border with Panama. The Darien Gap is filled with snakes, wasps, poisonous plants, insect-borne diseases, and also men: It is a base for armed rebels hiding from Colombian authorities. This last threat was to prove the most troublesome to Pelton: He and two companions were kidnapped at gunpoint by right-wing Columbian paramilitaries. He was lucky they had bothered to kidnap him rather than just kill him—minutes before, the paramilitaries shot to death four people in an ambush. During the next few days of captivity, Pelton was kept constantly on the move in the jungle and traded among different groups of rebels, before finally being held hostage at an abandoned cattle ranch. At the ranch, he didn't know if he would live or die on any given day, and faced the threat of instant execution.

This was not Robert Young Pelton's first brush with danger: In addition to the kidnapping, he has survived attacks of killer bees, Scud missiles, plane crashes, and an Algerian death squad. RYP, as he is known for his initials, is after all the world's most adventurous traveler: He is the author of the books *The World's Most Dangerous Places* and *Come Back Alive*. Eventually, he was freed from the Colombian kidnappers through the intervention of a Catholic priest. When asked if he would ever go back to the Darien Gap, given what happened, he replied without hesitation, "Absolutely...everything that is bad for you is in there. Which is, of course, what attracted me."

Pelton clearly loves risk, physical risk. He is more than just tolerant of it: He lives for it. Risk tolerance, as it is formally known, is also
a central concept in finance. A common idea is that people are either
risk seeking or risk averse across their lives, including their financial
decisions.

I caught up with Robert Young Pelton by email when he was in
Afghanistan to see what sort of risks he took with his investments:

"I don't do risks. I don't have a mortgage, don't use credit
cards, and live frugally," wrote RYP.

I wondered if he liked stocks. These are always touted as a safe
investment for the long run: Did he do much in terms of stocks or
stock picking? The response from RYP in Afghanistan:

"Nope. I used to work for Merrill Lynch as a mail boy."

As RYP shows, attitudes toward risks are, in fact, immensely complex and even contradictory. People may be risk loving in one area of
their life, but completely risk averse in another. We are inconsistent,
too, depending on moods or passing feelings. During the course of
the same day we may wake up ready to take chances, and end the day
willing to take no chances at all. The risk of going into a snake- and
rebel-infested jungle is clear. Financial risks are much less tangible.
Investing in the stock of the company you work for, for example, is
immensely risky because you can lose your job and your life savings at
once. Instead, many people perceive it as being unusually safe, in part
because it is so familiar.

Despite the significant challenges in identifying an investor's true
risk tolerance, the concept is a cornerstone of financial planning,
based on Markowitz's modern portfolio theory (discussed in the previous chapter). An investor's taste for the tradeoff between risk and
return guides his or her asset allocation. Any visit to a financial planner therefore begins with a short questionnaire designed to elicit the
investor's risk tolerance. This is typically a requirement as well: Planner's professional licensing organizations and compliance departments

demand it. The planner tabulates the results of a short multiple-choice questionnaire and pronounces the client risk seeking or risk avoiding and starts building a portfolio that corresponds to the clients taste for risk. Many financial planners who administer these tests don't buy into them, and I think their skepticism is warranted.

The Risks of Risk Tolerance Questionnaires

One problem with risk tolerance questionnaires is people will answer all sorts of questions about their opinions, regardless of the content of what is being asked. Take, for example, the experiment conducted by the researcher Sam Gill in 1947, asking people their views about the Metallic Metals Act. Participants were asked to choose among the following:

Which of the following statements most closely coincides with your opinion of the Metallic Metals Act?

- It would be a good move on the part of the U.S.
- It would be a good thing, but should be left to the individual states.
- It's all right for foreign countries, but should not be required here.
- It is of no value of all.

Seventy percent expressed an opinion one way or another. The majority selected the second choice—that it was a good thing but should be left to the individual states.

There is no such thing as the Metallic Metals Act. The experiment instead was to demonstrate how people can construct answers that sound plausible to researchers and more importantly to themselves, but really are nonsense. Risk tolerance questionnaires have a high risk of turning out this way. Additionally, a questionnaire completed in an office using a pen or pencil while you are calm misses out on how you would react under stress.

Part of the challenge is that risk in investing is not a topic most people are deeply familiar with or knowledgeable about. Psychologist Eldar Shafir of Princeton believes: "The average citizen doesn't know what is going on. This is not a trivial point. This was often true of those who signed sub-prime mortgage documents."

Identifying Your True Tolerance for Financial Risk

Understanding your financial risk tolerance is tough. For instance, after the crash, financial pundits proclaimed that investors' "risk tolerance" changed significantly. What is equally plausible is that clients were never made aware of the risks they were taking in the stock market. Their tolerance didn't change; their knowledge of risk did. If you go walking in the woods and a rattlesnake bites you, you will be more wary of going on such walks in the future. It's not because you are now suddenly less tolerant of rattlesnakes. You are just being sensible given the real risks involved.

Although assessing true tolerance for financial risk is a difficult task, it is not an impossible one. It requires a lot of research and effort to devise a meaningful test. At the very least, planners need to be more explicit about potential risks, and ask clients how they would feel if their assets lost 45% of their value. Would they still be interested in investing in the stock market? If investors had known more about the *possibility* of stock market crashes, before the one that occurred in 2008, they might have held much smaller allocations to equities.

Investors also need to be clearer about understanding the trade-off between risk and return. Often this tradeoff gets garbled in financial planning software to imply high risk *guarantees* high return. Increasing your allocation to riskier investment classes will certainly increase your likelihood of hitting otherwise unreachable investment targets. But these investments also have a higher likelihood of catastrophic loss, which is less clearly articulated.

Industry critics such as Boston University Professor Larry Kotlikoff label most financial planning software as a "con job" designed for sales not planning advice. The software doesn't clearly articulate the risk/return tradeoff. Instead, the true goal, Kotlikoff claims, is to direct users to high-yield but also high-risk asset classes because these give brokers the highest fees. Low-risk asset classes, such as treasuries, are ignored, because they have low returns and more importantly, low fees for brokers.

Given the immense complexity involved in risk tolerance, including the challenge of accessing our true attitudes toward risk as well as understanding the risk/return tradeoff, here is a way to make financial risk more tangible—by blowing up a balloon. BART, the Balloon Analogue Risk Task, is in fact a validated behaviorally based measure of risk tolerance. It was developed by Carl Lejuez, a psychologist at the University of Maryland. The basic idea is a participant is shown a deflated balloon on a computer screen. The participant is able to click on a pump, which blows up the balloon one click at a time. You get a nickel for each successful click. But if the balloon pops, you lose all your money. After 64 or so clicks, popping becomes increasingly likely, and at 128 clicks a certainty. Participants get to try using several balloons.

The balloon gets around people's problems guessing about how they would hypothetically react to the risk/return tradeoff by having them actually do an activity. The balloon illustrates that risk is a continuum. If you take too much risk, you can lose everything. But some risk is good. If you take no risk, the balloon remains deflated; you won't make any money because you aren't being risky enough. Maybe BART will someday become a mainstay of the financial planning profession, replacing today's inadequate risk questionnaires. Although BART uses a computer, you can use a real balloon to understand the same point and see how far you are willing to go before the balloon pops.

♦ ♦ ♦

In the next chapters, I turn from basic portfolio decisions to more advanced techniques—of ways to beat the market. I examine several strategies in detail. All are based on investor psychology and its impact on the market.

9

Deconstructing Stock Analysts

Stock analysts' recommendations move markets. During the tech bubble their pronouncements on the direction of a stock's price and buy recommendations were front-page news. After the tech bubble, analysts' recommendations became front-page news again, this time following investigations into their conflicts of interest, biases, and outright corruption. The Enron bankruptcy is a good example of the intellectual bankruptcy of some stock analysts: Only six weeks before the company went under, 15 of the 17 analysts covering the company rated the stock a "buy" or "strong buy."

Analysts are not completely useless, as you might conclude from this history (and Wall Street's multimillion-dollar settlements for false research practices). In fact, they are pretty good at what they do. Their recommendations have investment value—if you deconstruct their message to identify both their biases and what they are trying to say.

First the obvious biases: Most if not almost all recommendations are "buy." The ratio of "buy" to "sell" recommendations for stocks was along the lines of 10 to 1 in the early 1990s and since then has only became even more unbalanced. But where analysts' recommendations truly became unhinged from reality is for stocks their own bank is underwriting. Never is heard a discouraging word about these stocks from these analysts. During the IPO era, analysts affiliated with a bank doing an underwriting for a deal were 50% more positive than unaffiliated analysts. This wasn't irrational exuberance—it was just business. Analysts touted the stock to sell the IPO and support their company's investment banking business model.

The bias of underwriter analysts for a new IPO is now no longer so relevant. The market is savvier about analysts' conflicts of interests, and analysts themselves are more up front about these. There are new government regulations on the books, too. But really the whole issue is moot because the market for U.S. IPOs has dried up.

Additionally, the stock market has factored in many of these biases. If all analysts have a "buy" recommendation on a stock, and have held this opinion for a while, the market is well aware of this. There is no reason to buy the stock. Not necessarily because analysts are wrong but because the market has already made an adjustment based on the recommendations when they came out. You were the last to know.

Mainstream economists aren't surprised by the fact that analyst recommendations don't seem to add value. They are skeptical that anyone, including even a professional stock analyst, can beat the market. They view stock markets as "efficient." The price of a stock already incorporates all known information. There is no free lunch in terms of predictable returns.

Therefore, what is interesting is that despite these obvious drawbacks about analysts—the biases, the deeper theoretical concerns—investors can benefit from paying attention to their recommendations.

Kent Womack is a behavioral economist at Dartmouth who studies stock analysts, among other pursuits. He is also a competitive javelin thrower. He worked at Goldman Sachs for a long time before becoming an academic. He told me that this personal transition from Wall Street to academia is not usually a good thing for most people because the math in grad school is so "friggin' hard." But in his case, having a real-world background meant he knew what interesting questions to ask. And his interesting question was, "Do Wall Street analysts add investment value?"

Womack spent over a year thoroughly researching this question. He poured through the data to follow the actual movement of stocks that analysts had so confidently made forecasts about. Central to his research was identification in changes in recommendations, say from buy to sell or from sell to buy. He focused on market moves after brokers made upgrades or downgrades in opinions.

In response to the question about whether analysts are any good, Womack's answer from his research is a conditional yes. In the three-day period surrounding a change in status to a "buy," "strong buy," or "added to the recommended list," a typical stock rose 3% on average. Stocks with a sell recommendation fell 4.5% in the months following such a recommendation. These weren't short-term fluctuations in response to the power of the analyst—they persisted. The important thing is the typical stock continued to drift in the direction the analyst forecast, for as much as four to six months. Therefore, on average, the analysts are right. When an analyst downgrades a stock from a buy to a hold, that information is valuable in that the analyst tends to be correct because that stock, on a risk-adjusted basis, is likely to go down.

Before you rush out to buy a stock because it has a "strong buy" recommendation, you have to keep in mind that Womack is talking about changes in analysts' forecasts for a stock. As Womack emphasized to me, "This is the key factor that is valuable. It is not the level that is important, it is the *change* in the level. If eight or ten analysts already say buy, this is not useful information, this is not predictive of the stock outperforming. But if you see a stock going from a 'hold' to a 'buy,' or a 'buy' to a 'hold,' that is a good signal that stock will out- or underperform. Merely sorting stocks based on the consensus level of information isn't very valuable. Certainly, after transactions costs I can't find any value."

What is essentially going on is the stock market has already factored in the level of analyst recommendations. But it hasn't fully factored in the changes in the recommendations. It reacts, but not completely, not all the way. Womack puts it this way: "The market sees the news and waits to see how it will pan out. It doesn't overreact; in fact it under-reacts to the news." For a stock upgrade, say to a buy, most of the change will happen immediately, but even so, the average stock could still experience 2% excess return for the next three months. If the market had fully reacted right away, there would be no such drift in the following months.

This under-reaction of the stock market to changes is a common theme of behavioral finance. The market takes a while to fully incorporate new information. Take earnings "surprises." Investors see the earnings announcement and the stock will certainly reflect it, but it will continue to move in the direction of the surprise. This can continue for the next three quarters. Or take the case of a company reducing its dividend. The stock may fall—dramatically—but not all the downward move occurs right away. The market takes a while to fully react.

Says Womack, "You find that when the market receives either negative or positive news, it typically undershoots. It is fair to say this is widespread phenomenon, and that is the theme in my analysts research."

Even if the market under-reacts, it doesn't mean you have to. This is where the investment value of analysts' recommendations comes in. They are in fact telling you something valuable about the future direction of a stock, and you can move on this forecast before the rest of the market does. About half of the change in stock price will be instantaneous; it is the drift in the days and months afterward that is your profit window. Again, if analysts change their opinion to say a stock will outperform, on average the stock will continue to outperform for three to four months.

It helps to be a hedge fund that can trade immediately and aggressively on stock analysts' changes in recommendations. Having tiny transactions costs and being exempt from capital gains are necessary to make real money. Therefore, for individuals, trading this way isn't a money pump.

Even so, for individual investors, analysts' recommendations, or really, Womack's behavioral finance findings about how to analyze analysts' recommendations, are still useful. It means you have a better idea of what may happen to your portfolio. You have at least some signals of what the future may hold, even if you don't trade on the news. Additionally, Womack has found that negative movements following downgrades are larger than the upward movement on positive upgrades.

Investors still need to keep in mind that these findings work best for a whole portfolio and are about how stocks react *on average*. Any given stock still has a 40% chance of not responding the way analysts anticipate, even if the story holds most of the time. A broad portfolio is therefore necessary to pursue this strategy.

Womack's findings are important to investors, but they are also important to finance. They expose some of the cracks in the broad assumptions and conclusions of mainstream financial theory. Although the consensus has been that the market is "efficient" and all information is already priced in, the evidence of under-reaction to analysts' forecasts shows the market doesn't respond to or price in news instantaneously or adequately. Hence, there are trading opportunities. For investors, the storyline, or betting idea if you prefer, is quite simple. Womack puts it this way: "If analysts are changing their mind from hold to buy, the stock is likely to outperform in the next three months. But ignore analyst 'levels' of recommendations. All the investment juice is in the changes."

10

Value Investing: Behavioral Origins

In a fundamental sense, trying to beat the market is a zero sum game. The average performance of all portfolio managers can be no better than average. To look at it another way, there are two sides to every trade. One person is always wrong.

Value investing follows a formula: Invest in stocks that are undervalued or even cheap by several criteria, such as low P/E ratios, low price-to-cash-flow ratios, or low price-to-book ratios. These tend to be stocks with low growth rates in boring industries, small caps that get little attention, stocks with no glamour at all. In another words, the idea is to search for overlooked stocks, the ugly ducklings of the stock market. The value proposition—and proof—holds that these sorts of stocks consistently outperform the market portfolio and have lower risks than the market portfolio. This is one of the few investment strategies that has been shown to persistently outperform the market. The reason value investing works has everything to do with human behavior and our faulty financial intuition.

Value investing was first formalized as an idea by Benjamin Graham and David Dodd, professors at Columbia Business School, who in 1934 wrote the book *Security Analysis*. Warren Buffett was their student. He put their ideas into practice. His homilies usually have a value investing message. For instance, at the very bottom of the bear market in 1974, *Forbes* asked Buffett how he felt: "Like an oversexed guy in a whorehouse. Now is the time to invest and get rich," was his response. In contrast, at the height of the tech bubble, Buffett was widely criticized for not getting a piece of the tech action. To this he replied, in 1999, when everyone was tech crazy, "It means we miss a lot of very big winners. But we wouldn't know how to pick them out anyway. It also means we have very few big losers—and that's quite helpful over time. We're perfectly willing to trade away a *big* payoff for a *certain* payoff."

Today's foremost value investing theoretician is Bruce Greenwald, also at Columbia Business School, following in the footsteps of Graham and Dodd. He terms value investing a "massively successful" strategy, outperforming the market on average by 4% annually. Although he is by no means a behavioral economist, he relies upon a behavioral explanation for the success of the value proposition.

"The first thing you want to ask yourself in active investing is why are you on the right side of a trade for any stock," Greenwald tells me, "and value investing—looking for non-glamour stocks, or low P/E stocks, gives you an answer. It statistically puts you on the right side of trades on average. This is rooted in behavioral finance." Greenwald sees three psychological factors that best explain why certain stocks become undervalued.

First, as Buffett himself said, value stocks don't tend to have big payoffs. Their success is incremental; you won't strike it rich overnight. They are in every sense the opposite of lottery tickets. And people love lottery tickets. Lotteries are successful in every country in the world, despite their horrible odds as investments. Value stocks, unlike lottery tickets, or growth stocks, don't hold out the promise of a dream. Because they are boring, with real but limited growth, the market discounts them and they fall in price.

Second, as behavioral experiments have proven repeatedly, humans are loss averse. A loss is more painful than a gain is pleasurable. And not only to do value stocks not promise an outsized gain, they often do seem to have the real potential for some sort of immediate loss. A cloud hangs over these companies and stocks. Greenwald puts it this way: "Stocks that are cheap are ugly stocks, with depressing stories. People irrationally dump them because they want to dump the ugly stories."

HMO's are a good example of this sort of value stock. They once had a very positive financial story, and were seen as socially progressive too, a force for good. The idea of integrated healthcare that is an HMO, with doctors and hospitals and patients all members of one health organization, was first developed by the industrialist Henry Kaiser. He thought this would lead to healthier and happier workers, and he offered a type of HMO to workers building his Hoover dam. It was a successful experiment by every measure. Today, HMOs are seen as a force for bad. Their perceived function is to deny healthcare. They were attacked in Michael Moore's film *Sicko*. A reformed U.S. health system could someday eliminate them. Needless to say, with their uncertain future and unpleasant present, HMOs have become a value stock.

Finally, people are overconfident. For Greenwald, the link to value stocks is investors are overconfident a certain scenario will occur, and this applies to both the upside and the downside. We think a growth stock will continue to grow and a value stock will only continue to go down. Possible scenarios are interpreted as certain scenarios. When people think stocks are going to do well, they overbuy those stocks. And stocks that look bad, that might be facing trouble, are priced as if that trouble is certain.

Additionally, I think part of the success of the value proposition is related to our problems understanding statistics, and our preference for compelling stories over abstract statistical laws as the best explanation of patterns we see. Mean reversion alone may explain why value stocks improve and growth stocks fall back to earth. This statistical story may be the whole story. But our intuition has problem handling this abstract explanation, and so we mentally discount the likelihood of below-average stocks returning to average. We look for deeper meaning where there is none.

The success of value investing has been known for many years, since Graham and Dodd's book in the 1930s. Buffett and John Templeton's success as value investors isn't exactly secret. So why then hasn't the market arbitraged away this anomaly? Why isn't everyone a value investor? There are, of course, lots of rational reasons. It can take a very long time for cheaply priced value stocks to return to fair value. As I keep emphasizing, the stock market and investing are faddish, and cycle through value as well as growth crazes. Although Buffett didn't lose money because he sat out the tech bubble, it means he couldn't make it there either, and a lot of people got very rich through Internet stocks.

Also, before you get bitten by the value bug, keep in mind that value investing usually gets killed during severe market downturns. The success of value investing in the last decade, before the recent crisis, was driven largely by private equity managers who scoured the market for undervalued companies to snap up. If private equity becomes sidelined because of problems obtaining credit, value stocks won't have the same solid support levels.

Nonetheless, study after study proves value works. (Also, remember that value investing isn't buying stocks that merely look bad, it always means using some sort of formalized evaluation process to determine if stocks are underpriced.) To become a successful value investor, you have to overcome your hardwired aversions and intuitions. This isn't the story of Black Swans, anticipating some unimaginable, essentially unthinkable random event with huge consequences. Value investing is much easier and more predictable than that. All you have to do is find the cygnet everyone else has ignored and written off that will turn into a White Swan.

11

Timing Stocks

It's almost impossible to time the market. A few hedge funds did it successfully during the tech bubble, riding it both and up and down. A lot of hedge funds did it unsuccessfully during the credit bubble, riding it profitably on the way up only to be smashed to pieces on the way down. In general, almost no one can predict whatever they may claim, whether the Dow or S&P 500 will go up or go down, or when precisely the market will turn. Although everyone would like to know if it is a "good time to buy" because we are at a market bottom, or a "good time to sell" because we are at a market top, market timing, as any financial planner or Wall Street pro will tell you, is something to avoid.

But if you can't time the market, this doesn't mean you can't time individual stocks. There is an anomaly to the conventional wisdom: Under certain circumstances, the future direction of a stock is largely predictable, letting you know when it is a good time to buy or sell. Doing so involves watching the company in question's moves in the capital market: Whether it is betting against or in favor of its own stock. Technically known as the net stock issues anomaly, this technique is based on recent discoveries about stock price patterns following a corporation buying back its shares or issuing new ones. The "anomaly" is that these actions are a predictor of the future price of the stock. The basic facts are these: The price of stocks of companies buying back their shares, on average, tend to rise over time. The stocks of companies issuing new shares tend to fall.

Financial theory argues otherwise: You shouldn't be able to predict anything; it should all be factored into the *current* price of a
stock. But even Eugene Fama and Kenneth French, the two academics who created the market efficiency theory of modern finance, arguing that stock price movements are unpredictable, recently admitted:
"The anomalous returns associated with net stock issues...are pervasive; they show up in all [stock] size groups—micro, small, and big."
With even old-school finance types acknowledging there is something
to this, investors should start paying attention as well, even though
the anomaly is not widely known. For those interested in how it all fits
together, a company's decision to buy back or issue new shares is an
area where corporate finance (the company's decision to sell or buy
stock) meets capital markets (the market reaction) meets behavioral
finance. For those just interested in investing, the operative word for
the "anomaly" should instead be "opportunity," because this is one of
the few ways you are likely, though, of course, not guaranteed, to beat
the market.

The buyback anomaly is largely the discovery of three economists: David Ikenberry and Josef Lakonishok (both from the University of Illinois at Urbana Champaign) and Theo Vermaelen (a Belgian
economist now teaching at Insead, the business school outside of
Paris). I spoke to Vermaelen, who explained what is really going on
with buybacks, and how investors can profit from watching a corporation's moves regarding its own stocks. (This is distinct from the moves
of corporate insiders themselves, where personal considerations
rather than beliefs about undervaluation may be dominant. Executive
compensation is usually already in the form of company stock, so the
presence of this stock in their personal portfolio contains little information. The exception is a large amount of unexercised options which
may be revealing about a CEO's psychological profile; see Chapter
29, "CEO Hubris.")

"When companies buy back and repurchase their own stock, the
usual reason is because the firm believes the stock is undervalued.

The typical company buying back shares is a firm that has recently been 'beaten up' in the stock market," says Vermaelen. The beating has usually occurred because the company missed an earnings forecast. Analysts become gloomy about the company's prospects, extrapolating the short-term problems into the future. They downgrade the stock. These are often small companies with few analysts following them. But corporate insiders believe, or may even know, the problems are one-off events, short term not long term. Their stock may be down, but the company is not out. And so they see it as a good time for the company to buy back its own stock.

What is therefore occurring is a battle between management with a long-term view and analysts with a short-term view. Says Vermaelen, "The market is responding to analysts who focus on short-term performance. The focus on short-term performance may be the result of the use of earnings multiples to value companies. But this technical measure may sometime give the wrong picture in the long term, so the stock is mispriced, creating an opportunity for investors.

Examples of this mispricing included many energy and financial stocks during the Internet bubble. These weren't sexy at the time, so they were underpriced—and management knew it and bought back shares. And this time period also shows the flipside of the anomaly. Internet companies were issuing new shares—they knew their stocks were overvalued. We all know what happened to Internet stocks.

Issuing new shares is a signal from insiders that the market is too positive about the company's prospects, indicating it is a good time for investors to sell. The corporation is in some senses "shorting" its own stock—diluting it by issuing new shares. According to this logic, the biggest short trade during the tech bubble was AOL buying Time Warner, when AOL issued $200 billion of new equity to do the deal.

You shouldn't automatically conclude that corporate insiders are geniuses. Many people (with the notable exception of Jerry Levin, the CEO of Time Warner who oversaw the merger with AOL, selling his company for AOL stock) knew AOL was overvalued at the time. It's just the structure of the market and corporations themselves that allow them to take risks even hedge funds shy away from. If a hedge fund shorts a stock, believing it will go down, but in fact the stock goes up, the fund could be ruined. AOL didn't run this risk; it just issued new shares to take advantage of the market. If it bet the wrong way, that would have been unfortunate, but not financially ruinous. And as we know, AOL management bet the right way; its stock was overvalued. It cunningly timed the takeover of Time Warner at exactly the right moment. Therefore, corporations face less risks than investors trying to go short. "Perversely, the most aggressive arbitrageurs are corporations themselves, using market timing for their own stocks," Jeremy Stein, president of the American Finance Association, points out.

Even if investors avoid shorting stocks, they will run head first into a competing anomaly: momentum. (See the next chapter for more about momentum effects.) "Momentum works against buybacks," acknowledges Vermaelen. "The most undervalued buy-back stocks are firms that experienced large price declines in the previous six months, stocks with negative momentum." Buyback investors are busy buying undervalued shares. But momentum investors are busy selling them. As a result, in the year after the buyback announcement, no abnormal returns are observed. It is only in the long term that people see that the negative earnings surprises were just short-term problems.

And maybe this explains why more investors don't jump on buybacks. The pattern of stock returns doesn't *look* good. Investors have to put their faith into management, who have had already blown it in some big way that has driven the stock down, to turn the stock around. The buyback strategy presents additional psychological challenges to investors because of what it requires: patience.

"Investors aren't patient," observes Vermaelen. "Anything that is based on short-term responses can be arbitraged away. But here you have to be a long-term investor. Hedge fund investors, who want to do quick trades, find this boring. It isn't sexy. It's just buy and hold. But it works better than active short-term trading. It's why there aren't many buyback investors and the anomaly persists."

The good news is, for these exact same reasons, it is an easy anomaly to exploit in practice to make money. The strategy is simply to buy a set of stocks of corporations that are buying back their own undervalued shares. Hold the stocks for up to three years. After three years, this portfolio, Vermaelen claims, beats risk-adjusted measures of market return by up to 50%. However, you have to focus on purchasing shares that are likely to be undervalued. Together with Urs Peyer, his colleague from Insead, Vermaelen has developed an index that measures the likelihood that a buyback stock is undervalued. "If you picked a portfolio of 50 stocks with the highest undervaluation index at the beginning of each year, starting in 1992 and ending in 2004, you always beat the S&P 500 after three and four years." And it doesn't require active trading. That's the nice thing about this. Because it's a long-term strategy, you don't have rush into buying or selling stocks. Instead, you can leisurely build up your portfolio, indulging in everyone's basic propensity for inertia, and, with luck, watch the stocks grow.

12

Momentum

On May 4th, 1998, *The New York Times* front page contained a special report, "HOPE IN THE LAB: A Cautious Awe Greets Drugs That Eradicate Tumors in Mice." The article, by science reporter Gina Kolata, breathlessly claimed: "Within a year, if all goes well, the first cancer patient will be injected with two new drugs that can eradicate any type of cancer, with no obvious side effects and no drug resistance—in mice. Some cancer researchers say the drugs are the most exciting treatment that they have ever seen...."

Following this momentous news, the stock price of EntreMed, the biotechnology company with rights to this wonder drug described by Kolata, soared by over 500% reaching at one point $85.00 a share before dropping down. However, the special report was hardly a scoop. *The New York Times* hadn't actually broken any news. The alleged powers of Endostatin, the alleged wonder drug in question, had already been reported elsewhere previously. Months before, *Nature* magazine, which only has a tiny readership, had described Endostatin's potential ability to shrink tumors. The stock market largely overlooked the *Nature* article, despite the presence of stock analysts scouring research reports. When the *Nature* article first came out, EntreMed's stock price rose from $12.00 to $15.00. But it went no further than this. It took the front-page news of *The New York Times* to push the price to hysterical highs. Eventually EntreMed fell back to earth when *The Wall Street Journal* revealed Endostatin was not, in fact, the cure for cancer that everyone had been hoping for. EntreMed's stock declined to \$24.87, still much higher than before the positive press coverage.

The amazing rise and fall of EntreMed, first noted by economists Gur Huberman and Tomer Regev, shows that stock prices can move on many factors besides economic fundamentals. Media attention is crucial, too. In EntreMed's case, the alleged powers of Endostatin were already in the news, but just hadn't captured national attention—it took the "no new news" *New York Times* cover story to get the message out and launch EntreMed's stock price upward, even if it mostly ended in tears. EntreMed's story demonstrates the power of hype, of publicity, and how long it takes information to trickle out to the market and for the market to fully react, even though mainstream financial economics claims the reaction is instantaneous. And the rise of EntreMed's stock price is, among other things, a story of momentum.

Momentum

Momentum, in stock market terms, is the phenomenon that stocks that go up tend to keep going up. And stocks that go down keep going down. But momentum is deceptive, and the movements are subtle, only occurring for specific windows of time, and sometimes stopping altogether. The rise of EntreMed's stock price—characterized by two steps forward, one step back, with higher and higher spikes along the way before an eventual fall—shows the erratic patterns of momentum.

It's not exactly clear why stock prices exhibit momentum, but it is clear that they do, and momentum can form the basis for a very profitable investing strategy. Some studies have found that momentum stock picking strategies can produce above-market returns of 0.5% up to 1.5% a month.

"Here are the facts about momentum: There are price reversals at very short horizons, then positive momentum for 6 to 12 months, and then reversals again," explains Owen Lamont, a hedge fund manager and former finance Professor at the Yale School of Management. In simplest terms, what Lamont is describing is a stock showing momentum doesn't pursue a straight path upward. Instead, it zigzags up and down before eventually rising in value over a 6- to 12-month period.

"There are several possible explanations for momentum," Lamont continues, "many rooted in investor behavior." Although no one has ever come up with a fully satisfactory explanation of momentum, there are three basic theories. One is that "momentum" is merely the manifestation of investors' delay in reacting to earnings announcements. A second is that the slow spread of news accounts for momentum. And the third, and simplest, is that investors are chasing returns, driving stocks higher. These ideas can overlap.

For Lamont, the most compelling explanation of momentum is that the stock price patterns we are seeing are the result of investors "under-reacting" to earnings announcements. This accounts for the slow build in price rather than instant adjustment. Let's say IBM has an unexpectedly good earnings announcement. The market reacts, but only partially: Investors' inherent inertia causes the price of the stock not to fully reflect the good news. And then IBM has a second good earnings announcement a few months later. Again the stock goes up, but not as much as is warranted by the real financial picture. Eventually investors catch on. The price of the stock finally falls into line with the improved situation. "Investors are being continually surprised by earnings announcements, and momentum is consistent with their under-reaction," say Lamont.

Alternatively, most investors may just not be aware of the news about the company at all, until the story breaks on the front page of *The New York Times*. This slow dispersion of news, with investors not 'under-reacting' but simply being unaware, also could explain momentum. The rise and fall of EntreMed is consistent with this idea: A few investors learned about the power of Endostatin from early news articles, but *The New York Times* brought it to the attention of more investors, with the price building along the way as the news trickled out.

Or maybe momentum is just a case of "nothing succeeds like success." After all, we see similar experiences in the real world all the time. Some celebrities' careers start to snowball; their success brings on even more success; they have "momentum" while others are on a painful glide to the grave. Investors watch a stock going up, think it's hot, chase returns, and reinforce the trend by driving it higher before it all comes crashing down. Investors' simple extrapolation of past price trends into the future in this case actually pushes prices beyond their fundamental value.

Whatever may explain the momentum effect, it is one of the few ways for investors to beat the market. Because you know where the prices of certain stocks are heading, you know which stocks to buy or short. If you want to pursue a momentum strategy, timing is everything. In terms of implementation, the technique is to find the best performing stocks for the last half year or so, say the top 10%, and then buy and hold them for an additional short period of time. Advises Lamont: "Six to 12 months is the standard for screening. You screen on this past performance, and then you hold for one month."

Momentum strategies work better in bull markets than bear markets, and in December as opposed to January. Again, the momentum is for individual stocks, not the market for the whole, where momentum is much less pronounced. The December effect could exist because sophisticated investors are selling off their losing stocks for tax reasons, accelerating the downward slide. (In general, seasonality in the stock market is nothing new, but most seasonal patterns are now changing and possibly disappearing. For years insiders talked about the "January effect": that stocks tended to shoot up the first few days of January, from the 1st through the 5th. The argument behind this was not that the market "wanted" to start off the new year with a bang, but investors had harvested their tax losses in December and therefore needed to reinvest their cash in January, pushing stocks up. But just as the January effect has become widely known to investors, it has largely vanished. This is a case again in finance of things working until they stop, usually once they are well known. But even though it is well known, momentum, like value, keeps working.)

Combining Momentum with Value Investing

Momentum and value investing strategies appear to be polar opposites. Value investing involves trying to buy cheap securities that you think are lower than their true fundamental value. Momentum is the idea that stocks that are going up tend to keep going up regardless of their value. A value investor is likely to shun a momentum stock that is soaring upward, further and further away from its fundamental value, whereas for a momentum investor this trajectory alone makes it a tempting buy.

Although value investing and momentum investing are distinct strategies and in fact are negatively correlated, it is possible to look at them in combination. Could there be a way to pursue both at once? This idea has been investigated by Cliff Asness, Tobias Moskowitz, and Lasse Heje Pedersen. Asness runs AQR, the quantitative hedge fund based in Greenwich, Connecticut, for which Moskowitz and Pedersen consult in addition to their work as finance professors.

Their research has uncovered many previously unknown facts about both momentum and value.

One of their most basic and most surprising findings is that pursuing momentum or value strategies doesn't just work for U.S. stocks. The strategies can generate abnormally positive returns everywhere: in foreign stocks, currencies, commodities, even government bonds. Momentum occurs in many more asset classes than anyone previously realized or even contemplated. Says Moskowitz, "Momentum and value are big phenomena. When we started looking for them globally, we found them everywhere. They are ubiquitous."

Not only have they found evidence of momentum across the globe, the momentum is correlated. If U.S. stocks start showing strong signs of momentum, so do stocks in emerging countries. There is no obvious reason why this should be the case. Furthermore, when momentum works, value doesn't, and vice versa. That they seem to offset one another explains why momentum has never proven to be a successful investment strategy for Japanese stocks—it's because value works so well there. And, in the U.S., although momentum does badly in January, value strategies historically have performed quite well.

Adds Moskowitz: "Looking at a momentum or value in an individual market, say U.S. equities, you don't learn that much. But looking at the global economy, some patterns emerge. One seems to be related to global macro-economic risks. The other is liquidity." Liquidity, meaning easy cash and credit, seems to help value investors. When credit markets are illiquid, as in 2008, value investing gets destroyed. This might be because investors are having trouble getting the cash they need to buy value stocks, so these stocks keep dropping in value. Macro-economic risks tied to economic growth and the threat of a recession also affect the success of each strategy. During a recession, neither value nor positive momentum investing seem to work very well. Both are very sensitive to an extreme downturn.

I met with Lasse Pedersen in his NYU office to learn more about this research and its practical applications. The main conclusion arising from the research is you can be both a value *and* momentum investor, it doesn't have to be either/or. This new strategy is not widely practiced or even widely known. Until the recent findings, combining value with momentum investing seemed counterintuitive and even illogical because they are opposite strategies.

"The theme is in fact very simple," Lasse Pedersen patiently explained. "You buy stocks that look cheap on a value measure, but are beginning to come up, to show signs of positive momentum. Or you short overpriced stocks that are showing signs of momentum downwards." In another words, you look for stocks that have departed from fundamental value, with momentum the catalyst that is finally returning them to fundamental value.

Pedersen pointed out this value-momentum combo strategy works for bonds and currencies, too, suggesting it is not just a statistical anomaly of U.S. equities. He has examined the price patterns of currencies that rank high in terms of value, because they have been beaten down from their usual trading range, and also rank high in terms of positive momentum. Currencies that score highly in both dimensions are the most likely to quickly appreciate.

When I asked Pedersen how those of us outside of the hedge fund world can most easily implement the value-momentum combination in our own portfolios, here is what he suggested: "The approach is simple. Tilt your portfolio to stocks that have both—cheap stocks that now have movement and a catalyst that people are getting excited about." Also, you will need to diversify across many, many stocks; this approach is unlikely to work for just one or two securities. However, most of us don't have academic databases or research teams at our disposal identifying undervalued stocks that are beginning to show signs of momentum. How could we possible screen for stocks with these characteristics? Pedersen has an easy and inexpensive solution: Yahoo Finance.

13

The Ultimate Anomaly: Trusting Your Gut in Finance

The last few chapters have described ways to beat the stock market by doing the opposite of what your gut tells you to do, when everyone else is listening to theirs. This contrarian approach allows you to outperform the market and take advantage of various market "anomalies." These are profit opportunities at odds with theories of market efficiency, which argue they shouldn't exist.

In general, not trusting your intuition when it comes to financial markets is usually a good idea. The classic example is investors' stock market forecasts. The way most people make financial forecasts is completely natural: They just extrapolate from the present into the future. Although this feels right emotionally, it is usually wrong intellectually. There is a negative correlation between most investors' predictions and the true future direction of the stock market. (Note that this inverse correlation isn't strong enough that you can make money betting against investor sentiment.)

However, there are a handful of exceptions, anomalies to the "don't trust your gut in finance" idea. In these cases, trusting your gut is by far the best course of action. One area of financial markets where our intuition, even uninformed intuition, works well without too much deliberation is in predicting market volatility.

♦ ♦ ♦

Volatility—that is, the swings in market prices—isn't exactly a secret. It is easy to observe; you can see the changes from minute to minute. But what is more interesting is that short-term volatility is easy to predict. You don't need a complex model. An intuitive approach is usually sufficient.

The reason that your intuition works so well for observing and forecasting volatility is that it isn't random. Volatility comes in clusters. It is persistent. If markets are volatile today, they will be volatile tomorrow. It is similar to inflation in that volatility tends to last.

Although you can easily predict volatility in the blink of an eye based on recent market conditions, sadly you can't make money from this prediction. "Volatility is already embedded in options pricing," explains NYU economist Stephen Figlewski. If volatility is high, option prices are high. There is no easy way to trade on this information.

However, the long-term direction of volatility is not so easy to forecast, certainly not by intuition. It tends to revert to the mean, but no one knows when precisely. Some sophisticated traders now talk about volatility as an asset class. They take long or short positions on volatility, using complicated strategies and lots of financial engineering.

"Volatility is a number," adds Ser-Huang Poon of the University of Manchester Business School. "Some people are scared of this number. And other people want to trade it. And where there is demand in fluid markets, there is always some supply." It's really like betting on the weather. Traders write derivatives on the weather and invest in it, and the same is true of volatility.

These long-term strategies for trading and hedging volatility are very complex, and require financial engineering models and possibly derivatives and options. But for an investor worried about what they are seeing in terms of immediate stock market volatility, there are simpler approaches. If you can't handle huge market swings because they produce huge mood swings, then trust your gut and sit out the market for a while.

Part II
The Track, the Stock Market, and Other Types of Gambling

Our gut instincts and snap judgments don't just lead us astray when it comes to investing: They also cause problems when it comes to gambling or when considering different "gambles" in sports strategies and horse betting. Part II of this book examines common intuitive mistakes when it comes to these sorts of real-life gambles. It culminates with a behind-the-scenes look at Las Vegas and the way casinos understand exactly how gamblers think.

I begin with a deeper examination of intuition—how it functions and its predictable biases.

14

Let's Talk about Linda: More About Our Intuition

Although we have two decision systems at our disposal—one analytical and slow, the other intuitive and fast—we live most of our lives on autopilot dominated by the latter. This is true of our financial decisions as well. Given that intuition is behind 90% of our judgment, let's delve a bit deeper into it and how it really works. So let's talk about Linda.

Linda is 31 years old, single, outspoken, and very bright. She majored in philosophy. As a student she was deeply concerned with issues of discrimination and social justice, and also participated in antinuclear demonstrations.

What do you think is more probable?

1. Linda is a bank teller.
2. Linda is a bank teller and is active in the feminist movement.

Eighty-five percent of people asked this question chose number 2, that Linda is a bank teller and also active in the feminist movement. But in terms of probability this makes no sense. Being a feminist bank teller is just a subset of being a bank teller. Overall there are more bank tellers in total than ones who happen to be feminists. Linda has a greater chance of being a bank teller than being a feminist bank teller, because the first doesn't rule out the other.

The Linda problem—actually a psychological reasoning test—is notoriously challenging, even controversial. The original question asked of participants was more difficult: There were a lot of filler questions to throw people off from the key statistical measures being tested. Even when the correct answer was explained to him, scientist Stephen Jay Gould had problems with Linda: "I know [the right answer], yet a little homunculus in my head continues to jump up and down, shouting at me—'But she can't just be a bank teller; read the description.'"

I think part of what makes the Linda problem so difficult is we usually make assessments of people *intuitively* based on fleeting impressions. This usually works well. Novels don't have to explain every detail of a character—a few words give us all we need to know. Similarly, when Linda Ronstadt sings "You're no good, you're no good, you're no good, baby you're no good," we never know who "baby" actually is, let alone the probabilities of the reasons why baby is bad, but this isn't a problem. Less is more than giving us all the boring details. We get it.

In the Linda problem, we are being asked to make assessments of people *statistically*, which requires analytical thought, forcing us to override our intuition, which normally suffices here. We aren't used to thinking about people using our slower, analytical decision system. There is something unfamiliar, even unnatural about this. Our wires get crossed. We can acknowledge the right answer while still having trouble letting go of the intuitive answer, even though it is wrong.

◆ ◆ ◆

The Linda "problem" was originally devised by the psychologists Daniel Kahneman and Amos Tversky. These two Israelis were interested in the psychology of intuition, particularly how our intuition handles statistical information and makes choices. Their research program into intuitive judgments and choices culminated in a Nobel Prize and formed the basis for behavioral economics.

In his Nobel Prize lecture in 2002, Daniel Kahneman took a look back. (Amos Tversky died in 1996 of melanoma, so the prize was awarded to Kahneman alone.) Said Kahneman, "Our first joint article examined systematic errors in the casual statistical judgments of statistically sophisticated researchers. Remarkably, the intuitive judgments of these experts did not conform to statistical principles with which they were thoroughly familiar. We were impressed by the persistence of discrepancies between statistical intuition and statistical knowledge, which we observed both in ourselves and in our colleagues."

Their experiments identified specific biases in thinking when it comes to numbers and probability. People don't make rational decisions, which anyone might have guessed, but we fail to do so in predictable ways. We tend to rely upon heuristics, or rules of thumbs, when facing complicated problems. The Linda problem involves the "representative heuristic." Linda represents a feminist bank teller more than she resembles the standard image of a bank teller, so we jump to conclusions about who she is—a conclusion that is wrong in terms of probabilities. Heuristics dominate our judgments when it comes to making quick choices. Kahneman and Tversky identified three heuristics at first, and then expanded the list to about ten. They gave them catchy or at the very least academic sounding names, such as "anchoring" and "representativeness." In anchoring, we start our reasoning with some number, and then move from there upward or downward. A lawyer tells a jury his client deserves ten million dollars. The jury awards half that, but they started with the number he suggested as their anchor in reasoning, for no rational reason. There are many, many other widespread biases. Research psychologists are constantly discovering new ones, while debating the meaning and precise contours of each one, as well as the exact mental processes involved.

Although you may feel intuitively you aren't subject to these biases, and also won't be taken in by the next financial fad, consider the following: After a plane crash, everyone overestimates the risks of plane crashes. This is formally known as the "availability heuristic," which means certain examples are more available to our minds,

prominent in our thinking after recent news, leading to errors in esti-
mating their probability of occurrence. Following the crashes in the
real-estate and credit-market bubbles, savvy investors were on the
lookout for new bubbles everywhere, under every rock and behind
every tree. Wall Street insiders were certain they had spotted new
ones emerging in U.S. treasuries and possibly the dollar. These
investors may have thought they were being hyper-rational and hard
headed, but in fact were in the grip of the availability heuristic, and
had become overly sensitive to bubbles while ignoring other financial risks.

The various heuristics are now widely discussed in the financial
press, even though their names are a mouthful. What is left out of the
discussion is they are just a part (though a big part, of course) of Kahneman and Tversky's larger research effort into understanding "intuition."

One recurring theme in this research, and, in fact, its starting
point, is that experts are prone to these same sorts of intuitive errors
in judgment as everyone else. This is something to keep in mind the
next time an investment expert pontificates on the future direction of
the stock market or a Wall Street CEO explains why the next time it
will be different.

Radiology is an example of an entire field particularly vulnerable
to expert mistakes. When reading X-rays, radiologists rely heavily on
first impressions to know if something is wrong. This is called the
"Gestalt approach." It works, but not always. In one experiment testing the accuracy of Gestalt interpretations, different radiologists were
all shown the same X-ray. They disagreed with each other about the
diagnosis about 20% of the time. When the same radiologists were
shown the same X-ray twice, but not told it was the same, 10% of
them disagreed with themselves and offered a new diagnosis. The
radiologist conducting this experiment, Dr. James Potchen of Michigan State University, then showed radiologists X-rays of a patient
missing his left clavicle. He told them to screen for a serious illness,

but didn't mention the clavicle. Sixty percent didn't notice anything was wrong.

The most interesting finding was how the radiologists rated their own judgments—they had almost no self-doubts. They thought their clinical skills and accuracy were terrific, even if they were terrible. No matter how wrong they were, the radiologists were completely confident they were right. This particular study is not an illustration of statistical errors but of the widespread human trait of overconfidence. This finding of overconfidence is a consistent theme in behavioral economics. CEOs are overconfident that mergers and acquisitions are a good idea, though they rarely are. In economics, "overconfidence" is sometimes used to describe our certainty that past trends—such as rising housing prices or, alternatively, falling housing prices—will definitely continue in the future.

Human tendencies and personality traits such as overconfidence are a source of biased decisions in addition to heuristics. We are shortsighted in our decision making: We generally prefer a small amount of something right now to a larger amount in the distant future. The most striking trait has to do with our feelings about gains and losses. Gains are pleasurable, of course, but losses hurt a *lot* more. We don't evaluate them equally. Kahneman and Tversky were even able to put a number on it: Losses have about twice the impact. And this has real impact on our behavior. We will go to great lengths to avoid losses.

Kahneman and Tversky formalized these ideas into something they called "Prospect Theory." They described different gambles as different "prospects" and hence came up with this name for the theory of how we evaluate risky alternatives. Also, allegedly, they thought the name sounded like something that could catch on. It has. Prospect Theory is extraordinarily influential in economics and has many interesting features. One is that we find losses so intolerable we are willing to take risks if we are in a hole to get back to even. Gamblers who are down are likely to double down to get back to even. They won't walk away and take the loss. But when we are ahead, we don't have the same urgency to keep taking risks. We have no emotional problem with locking in gains and taking our chips off the table. In essence, our response to gains and losses is asymmetric. Prospect Theory explains a lot of our behavior when it comes to investing as well as gambling, behavior that is very different from that predicted by mainstream economics.

◆ ◆ ◆

Would you take the following gamble?

1. Heads you win $80, tails you lose $20 dollars.

Most people will take that gamble. But how about this one?

2. You have to pay $20 first. But if it's heads you now win $100. If it's tails you win nothing.

Almost no one will take the second gamble.

These hypothetical gambles were posed to me by Shane Frederick, who teaches at the Yale School of Management and is at the forefront of contemporary decision research. He asked me what I thought. I truthfully told him that even thinking about these gambles made my head hurt, but aside from this problem, my first impression was the first gamble was a better deal.

The odds of the two bets are, of course, exactly the same. In both cases you end up with $80 if it is heads and lose $20 dollars if it is tails. But in the second bet, you have to pony up $20 to play, even if the gamble's payoff means you end up in exactly the same place as in the first bet.

Frederick, along with his colleague Nathan Novemsky, has been puzzling for some time over why people respond differently to the two gambles. He conjectured, "The sticking point for most people may be that in the second bet you seem to face the risk of losing twice. First, you lose the 20 dollars you shell out, and then you risk losing the coin flip, too. You have paid for the opportunity to lose, which people consider especially aversive."

The bigger puzzle, Frederick argues, is why people would ever turn down either gamble. Both are good bets. He describes this decision as pathologically risk averse and an example of poor judgment. Says Frederick, "People see problems too narrowly, and exaggerate the importance of this particular outcome in a very long life of effectively similar gambles." This narrowness in thinking, demonstrated in this experiment, is something that recurs again and again in the wider world of economic decision making. We don't see the bigger picture.

This vulnerability to being misled by different descriptions of the same gamble is known as a "framing effect." The second bet is framed as riskier because we have to put down money first. Framing effects influence our decisions, even if they make no material difference to the outcome. For instance, in one of his experiments Frederic asks people if they would like $100 now or $150 in six months. Most people want the money today. Then he changes the "frame" to, Do you want $100 now or $150 on a specific date two months from now, say, August 3rd? Most people will delay when this language is used. The specific date in two months diverts our attention to the future. We focus on that date, influencing our choice.

Frederick's newest area of research is exploring why we are so vulnerable to these intuitive mistakes. Kahneman and Tversky's original research identified various heuristics. It didn't fully explain why we don't ignore them when they clearly give us a wrong answer. Why don't we overrule intuition? Why do we give into to our first impressions rather than relying upon slow analytical thinking when it is called for? Frederick has a provocative answer as to why some people are more likely to make these sorts of mistakes than others. He claims it essentially comes down to IQ.

First, which of the following would you prefer?

- $500 for sure or a 15% chance of winning $1,000,000?

Frederick has posed this question to thousands of people across America. Most (a little under two-thirds) say they would take the sure

$500 over the gamble. This is true of people who are rich or poor, young or old. The majority of people just go for the $500. Frederick says this preference is simply "insane." He argues, "The expected value of the gamble is not just higher, it is 300 times higher, and $500 just isn't enough money to make a difference, even if you're poor."

Frederick provides evidence that preference for the gamble is very highly correlated with IQ (and not that highly correlated with age or wealth). However, he claims the results are not merely a matter of getting confused by the numbers. When he clarifies the odds and spells out the expected payoffs of $500 versus $150,000, the results are largely unchanged. He believes people with low IQs have a mental "coarseness" when evaluating different levels of wealth. Regarding the choice in question, Frederick says, "People who take the $500 usually justify it along the following lines: 'Wow, five hundred dollars is a lot of money, and it is a sure thing. One million dollars is also a lot of money, but I probably won't get it.' They don't appreciate the magnitude of the difference, the length of life, how little $500 will really matter in the long term, and so on. For all these things, intellectual ability helps."

He has also found people with higher IQs are more prone to gamble, even when the difference in potential payoffs is much smaller than $150,000 versus $500. And higher IQ participants exhibit much less marked differences toward reacting to gains and losses as described by Prospect Theory. They aren't as vulnerable to the intuitive errors that Kahneman and Tversky describe.

You could argue that some people have different preferences, and this determines liking or not liking different gambles. Some people like vanilla ice cream, and some people prefer sure bets. IQ doesn't explain all behavior, and as Frederick will acknowledge he doesn't yet understand how intelligence mediates these differences. But the fact remains that people with higher IQs in these gambling experiments make different choices (and Frederick thinks better choices) than subjects with lower IQs. As Frederick puts it, "I wouldn't necessarily let Einstein choose my dinner (a matter of 'pure' preferences), but I might let him manage my money (a mixture of 'preferences' and 'understanding')."

Fair enough, but a word of warning to Professor Frederick: Isaac Newton, the Einstein of his time, lost a vast fortune in the South Sea bubble.

Other Biases: Mood and Money

The biases in the way we reach the decisions that Frederick describes are hardwired in our brains. But fleeting emotions are important, too. How you are feeling—angry, fearful, or blue—affects your judgment. When you are in a good mood, you make different decisions from when you are in a bad mood. And certain emotions are associated with certain types of economic decisions. In particular, when people are angry they are willing to take on more financial risk. When people are sad, they don't feel they can handle financial risks. And when people are miserable, they aren't miserly. People who are feeling blue are willing to spend more money than those in a better mood.

These findings come from the research of Professor Jennifer Lerner, who runs the "emotion and decision-making lab" at Harvard. Lerner is a pioneer in the emerging field that investigates how emotional and social factors influence judgment and decision making. Much of her research attempts to understand and predict the influence of specific emotions on specific consumer decisions. This is a newer area of decision research and is yet another avenue of departure from the rationality assumed in economic models. A central idea is that emotions carry over into new, unrelated situations from the ones driving the mood. Moods spill into economic decisions.

In one of her experiments, Lerner first tries to make people sad. She does this by showing participants a sad video clip from *The Champ* where a boy's mentor dies. A control group is put in a neutral mood by viewing a neutral movie (from a mood perspective): a *National Geographic* special about the Great Barrier Reef. Also, Lerner evaluates participants' "self-focus" by noting how many times they use the words "I," "me," and "myself" in an accompanying essay she asks them to write.

Lerner then asks participants from both groups how much they would pay for something, in this case a new water bottle, a sporty type used in fitness clubs. Sad people will pay more for the bottle, $2.56 on average, a lot more than the 56 cents from the control group. People who were sad and very self-focused tended to be the biggest spenders.

What is interesting is the sad group claimed the video clip didn't affect their spending decisions. They weren't consciously aware they were still feeling down after the clip. Nor were they aware they were willing to spend more on the water bottle than people in a neutral mood.

Why exactly do sad, self-absorbed people spend more? One possibility is they are engaged in an unconscious form of mood repair. However, Lerner, and her co-authors in the research paper "Misery Is not Miserly" propose "that sad and self-focused individuals spend more on commodities than other people do because they seek self-enhancement." Because of their bad mood, they have devalued themselves and their possessions. Everything looks expensive compared to their diminished sense of self, and buying things boosts their self-worth.

Whatever the underlying cause for the change in spending behavior, it is still inconceivable under traditional economic theory. People are supposed to be rational and not subject to unconscious mood effects.

Lerner's research helps explain the strange shopping phenomenon observed in Manhattan the day Lehman Brothers failed. The expensive boutiques lining Manhattan's upper Madison Avenue were jammed with shoppers and had one of their best days in history. One possibility is that bankers' wives were rushing out to go on one last binge before their husbands cut off their credit cards. But maybe the wives were simply depressed and trying to shop back their self-esteem. As the saying goes, when the going gets tough, the tough go shopping.

Other Biases: Inertia

Perhaps the most pervasive bias that rules our lives is inertia. Newton's First Law of Motion (the law of inertia) holds that "an object at rest remains at rest, and an object in motion remains in motion unless acted upon by an outside force." The physics definition applies to human behavior, and is all too evident as we lounge on the sofa without the energy to get up or even to change the channel. Inertia characterizes the way we make our investment decisions, too.

Here is a dramatic thought example of inertia. Christopher Hsee, a behavioral scientist at the University of Chicago Business School, asks students if they will hold onto a stock that has lost 50% of its value in the last three months. Most say they are reluctant to sell and will keep the stock. This isn't particularly surprising or interesting.

But then Hsee asks his students to imagine that a cat jumps on their keyboard, and inadvertently sells these same shares. How will they react? Will they buy back the shares they were so reluctant to sell? Would you? Almost no one will. The inertia effect is too powerful, even though the investment choices have been made by a cat.

The History of Behavioral Economics

Traditional economics had little room for these psychological insights. Individuals in markets were assumed to be rational and have equal access to information. The result is economists believe markets should work smoothly on their own, with little need for guidance or regulation. Economists used these simplifying assumptions to build formidable mathematical models (and also indulge in their own psy-chological problems of "physics envy," that is, wishing their social sci-ence had mathematical fundamentals like physics). However, if these easy assumptions aren't met, suddenly economic models don't work so well in the real world. Traditional economics starts looking like an empty fortress, unable to explain investor or market behavior.

Economics had at times flirted with some behavioral ideas. Keynes wrote of "animal spirits," spontaneous human optimism that drives economic cycles. Harry Markowitz, the father of Modern Port-folio theory, noticed our asymmetric reaction to gains and losses. And Herbert Simon developed a theory of "bounded rationality," acknowl-edging that even rational people had to work within boundaries of time and information constraints when making a decision. But these departures from full rationality are few, and more importantly, eco-nomics hadn't found a way to formally model this sort of research (an issue which still hasn't been satisfactorily resolved).

The economist Richard Thaler, who had collaborated with Kah-neman and Tversky, changed all this, and economics along with it. Thaler injected Kahneman and Tversky's ideas about the psychology of decision making into economics, giving rise to the new field of behavioral economics.

Success has many fathers. The first generation of behavioral economists working alongside Thaler included Robert Shiller, who focused on macro-economics; Thaler's student Werner De Bondt; the psychologist Paul Slovic; and the team of Hersh Shefrin and Meir Statman of the University of Santa Clara. This generation was fol-lowed by a second and even third generation of behavioral econo-mists, many interviewed in this book and known to the general public. The field is now mainstream. Not everyone is a behavioral economist, but most leading economists are familiar with the field's literature and conclusions.

Although behavioral insights are taken for granted today, in its early years, the field was subject to harsh criticism from other economists.

These debates were not just academic. Their outcome would influence the way the rest of the world now thinks about economic processes, booms and busts, bubbles and crashes.

The wider world was very interested, even from the start. Meir Statman, who was present at the beginning, remembers a quick talk he gave in 1981 to some Lockheed executives about Prospect Theory. "I discussed the notion that people are reluctant to realize losses, and how that connects to selling stocks. It also connects to terminating a money-losing corporate project. Once they're started, these projects can take on a life of their own, and corporations are reluctant to shut them down." As an example, Statman pointed to Lockheed's own L1011 aircraft. This was an albatross around the company's neck. The three-engine jet was unable to compete with Boeing aircraft. Although it was a money-losing operation, Lockheed couldn't seem to let go, as Prospect Theory predicted.

Flying back home the next day, Statman stopped at a newsstand at the airport. The business headline was that Lockheed had decided to terminate the L1011. More interesting was the stock market's reaction: Lockheed's stock price soared. Behavioral economics, developed in classrooms and based on experiments using undergraduates, held lessons for the real world.

The following chapters examine other areas where behavioral economics applies well in the real world outside of finance, most notably in explaining gambling and sports strategy behavior. This parallels the history of behavioral economics itself, which from its early days studied decisions in these areas as metaphors for investing.

15

Why Investors Bet on Long-Shot Horses

The most persistent mistake in horse betting is known as "the favorite long-shot bias." This is the tendency to over-bet long shots and under-bet favorites. The true chance of the long shot horse winning is much worse than the odds at the track suggest. The payoff from a long shot may be 100 to 1, but the true odds may be closer to 200 to 1.

Gamblers seem to love long shots, even though the returns are remarkably dismal. The favorite long-shot bias has been observed for over 50 years in the U.S., England, and Australia, (though strangely less so in Hong Kong or Japan). Based on the outcomes of over five million races in the U.S., the average bet on a long-shot horse (with odds of 100 to 1 or greater) lost 60 cents for every dollar. In contrast, betting on the favorite in every race lost only five cents a dollar.

Try it. Go to the track. See what happens if you keep betting on the long shot. You will find, according to Justin Wolfers, a professor at Wharton Business School, "by betting on long shots you are likely to lose a lot of money."

Wolfers may currently be a professor but he has a long history at the track. He was formerly a bookie in his native Australia (a legal occupation). "I'm an Australian. We will bet on two flies crawling up a wall," says Wolfers. He planned to make bookmaking his career, but after being fired (he says for "excessive cockiness"), he went to college instead. Wolfers put himself through school by continuing to practice bookmaking on the side. He only gave up the practice when he went to work for Australia's Central Bank and then to graduate school in economics at Harvard.

"Being a bookmaker made me a better economist," Wolfers told me. "It made me think about markets and probabilities." Although the track is certainly a nontraditional market, it has similarities to being in a trading pit, with uncertain outcomes, real money at stake, and the forces of supply and demand determining prices.

Today Wolfers still returns occasionally to the track, but now only in the guise of an academic: He takes students from his business school class on Behavioral Economics and Prediction and Sports Betting Markets. His interest is not in making money for himself, it is in explaining anomalies and puzzles of the sports-betting markets. A central one for horseracing is, if long shots are such a statistically bad bet, why do people keep betting on them?

One possibility is romantic: Gamblers love the risks involved and think the big potential payoff makes a long shot worth it. The dream of a big win overwhelms the near certainty of a likely loss. The other, more mundane possibility is gamblers don't really understand the odds—they just don't get it.

In addition to a long-shot bet on a single horse, racing has similar long odds bets known as "exotics." These include an exacta (picking which horses will come in first and second in a race) and trifecta (betting which horses will come in first, second, and third, in exact order). To make these exotic bets, people have to calculate the odds for different horses involved as well as for the overall combination. Usually these high-ranked horses have much more manageable and understandable odds, say 4 to 1, of placing first or second, even if the overall exotic bet has very long odds.

In an ingenious piece of economics research, Wolfers was able to test which motive was driving gamblers' behavior by looking at long shots but also exotic bets. To do so, he and Erik Snowberg, one of his students, examined the data from *all* six million horse starts in the U.S. between 1992 and 2001. Teasing apart the results of exotic bets, they found gamblers could more or less correctly understand the odds of each individual component. These were in a low range (say, 4 to 1 or 6 to 1). It was when it came time to put together the bets into complex exotics that gamblers ran into trouble. Wolfers argues humans aren't well calibrated to be able to statistically evaluate long odds (say, 100 to 1 or 200 to 1). Our intuition can't fully comprehend odds in this range and make useful calculations or comparisons.

So when it comes to single bets on very-long-shot horses, gamblers aren't driven by a dream or a love of risk, but rather by a misunderstanding of the odds. As Wolfers and Snowberg write, "Behavioral theories suggest that cognitive errors and misperceptions of probabilities play a role in market mis-pricing.... People are systematically poor at discerning between small and tiny probabilities, and hence price both similarly." The favorite long-shot bias has nothing to do with belief in the underdog and everything to do with our faulty intuition when it comes to dealing with large numbers.

If most gamblers systematically overestimate the probability of a long shot winning, can you make money off their predictable errors? That is, once you are aware that others are prone to the favorite long-shot bias, can you exploit their mistake? The answer is no. Wolfers has found that any differences in odds are too tiny, and the track gets a cut, too, eliminating any profits. The only true savings that will accrue to gamblers aware of this bias will result from changes to their own behavior: They will stop betting on long shots and start betting on favorites. Instead of losing 60 cents on every dollar they will lose only five cents on the dollar.

But this begs the question of why people are betting on horses at all? Betting on long shots is a bad bet, but betting on favorites is still a money loser. Betting randomly at the track loses on average about 16 cents on the dollar. What is going on in people's calculations? Maybe they have a kink for horseflesh. Or feel they have a sixth sense. Or they may find a day out at the track is "entertainment." But gambling every day?

One way to find out is to ask them. Professional gamblers don't use the word "gambling" to describe their favorite activity or themselves. "Investing" is the preferred term. The serious habitués of the track think of themselves as investors. They are there to win. And they believe they *will* win money, with their "investment" research (knowledge of horses, jockeys, track conditions, history) providing the edge. And they are now assisted in their efforts through computer programs, which are constantly crunching numbers, looking for that edge.

Sound familiar? Wall Street, too, is populated by "investors" busy trying to spot any mispricing and find profit opportunities. These investors are also certain they have an edge. There are, of course, differences: You could argue the stock market is more socially useful than the track; it allows companies to raise capital and investors to retrade stocks. And there are sociologically differences, too. The track is now largely a charmingly old-fashioned institution, populated by Damon Runyon characters with too much time on their hands. (Runyon, obsessed with the underworld and gambling, was a cynic who maintained a very realistic sense of the true odds involved in most gambles and other activities, too. In one short story, his character Sam the Gonoph says, "I long ago come to the conclusion that all life is six-to-five against.")

Despite these distinctions, the sheer volume of trading on Wall Street points to its essential similarity to the track. According to standard, rational economics, you would see very little trading by investors, who would rebalance their portfolios once in a while and draw down their wealth as they age. That wouldn't account for very much turnover. But the daily turnover in stock markets is immense, much larger than these rational or functional motives could explain. Similarly, given that betting on horses is a negative sum activity, you wouldn't expect people to play this game at all, much less the degree to which committed gamblers "play the ponies." Some other impulse is at work, some not fully rational impulse, a sort of thirst. Says Wharton professor Wolfers, "In both domains people think they are investing. But they are actually gambling."

16

Gambling Continued:
Stories We Tell Ourselves

A man I will call Al "Dogs" is a luminary in certain Brooklyn old-school gambling circles. ("Dogs" comes from all the time he spent at the dog track.) Al's claim to fame is his extraordinary win at the Kentucky Derby a few years ago. On a single $100 bet on a trifecta, he cleared a million dollars. His life changed. Al Dogs moved out to the "island" (Long Island) and is the first to buy drinks for friends. The Governor of New Jersey once invited him to open a race.

Al remains a very heavy gambler. He is constantly at the track, including his old weakness: the dog track in South Florida, a sociological low. Al doesn't discuss his losses, only his wins. And over the years, the losses may have been substantial, easily larger than the wins. But despite the real financial picture, Al to his friends, but more importantly to himself, is a winner, *the* big winner, because of that day at the Derby.

We tell ourselves stories about our wins and losses. During the worst days in the panic of '08 every hedge fund manager I saw on TV or was unlucky enough to meet in person told the same story: "We've made a lot of money this week. It's my friends that I'm worried about." They would then add, almost as a footnote, "Of course, we are down for the year." Part of this misrepresentation is marketing, but it could also be a case of misremembering. One huge win is easier to remember than death by a thousand small cuts of losses at the dog track. And even if we didn't win we tell ourselves we could have, if only....

If only I had gone to law school I would be happier, we might tell ourselves. Or if only I *hadn't* gone to law school I would be happier. It is easy to imagine an alternative state of the world. And it is easy to blame ourselves, to regret not having achieved this alternative state. This selective self-storytelling is technically known as creating "counterfactuals."

These ruminations can cause great self-pain when it comes to investing. We kick ourselves more for actions that turn out badly than inactions that turn out badly, mistakes of doing something over mistakes from doing nothing. In a classic early behavioral finance experiment, people were given two scenarios: You own a stock and can keep it, or you have the opportunity to switch to another stock. In the experiment, both stocks went down. But the people who switched felt worse, much worse.

By changing stocks, people were now more vulnerable to feeling regret. Investors felt more responsible. Perhaps this accounts for our overall inertia when it comes to investing, our fear of departing from the way things are now, of being mocked for our efforts.

But over time, the story changes. We regret *not* doing things as our life goes past. We start blaming ourselves for inaction, not action. Not buying that Microsoft stock. In the end, regret is a two-edged sword.

Jim Sherman is a psychologist at Indiana University. He studies stories gamblers tell themselves about why different outcomes occurred, outcomes that are in fact determined by pure chance. Although he studies gambling, his work has particular importance for investors. Says Sherman, "If you think about the stock market as gambling, which I do, our work has real significance."

Sherman's psychological experiments often involve horse betting. In one, a set of gamblers is allowed to attend an actual race. They see the track, the jockeys, and the horses. And they are given information about the race history of the horses and the jockeys—they can really do their research if they want to. Another set of gamblers is provided with much less information: only the odds involved, the horses, and whether a horse won or lost. No other details are provided. This second group is not allowed to see the race or assess the horseflesh.

It turns out that people who watch the race and got specific information were not better gamblers than the people who were told nothing. But they *thought* of themselves as better decision makers. From the additional information they were provided, they were able to generate complex stories about what was going on. And they could create excuses ("counterfactuals") if their horse lost. The net result of all their mental handiwork is that although their likelihood of winning didn't improve, their propensity to gamble and keep betting on horses shot up.

Says Sherman, "People are always trying to come to grips with bad outcomes. These counterfactuals have benefits in terms of emotions." People have tremendous trouble understanding randomness. There is an innate need for control and to make sense of a senseless situation.

In terms of investing, the more specific information you get about a product or company, the more you think you really know about it. Psychologically speaking, it also allows you to generate more counterfactuals about the company and the direction of its stock price. And you think better of yourself. You *feel* more prepared, even if you have no true greater insight into the statistical reality of the situation.

For Sherman, this accounts for the massive appeal of playing financial markets, as opposed gambling on games of chance such as roulette. Says Sherman, "The reason financial markets are so popular as opposed to pure gambling is people really believe they have control over what happens to their investments in the sense they can make good decisions and aren't random."

This is also seen in the pronouncement of stock market strategists who are always able to come up with some reason for stock market moves. They can look at the same data and create complete contradictory explanations on market moves—even during the course of the same day, by the same analyst. Stock "analysts" craft stories that appeal to our (and their) intuition, avoiding the brutal reality that the market moves have no more meaning and are not much more predictable than the turn of the roulette wheel.

Hot Streaks in Basketball

This larger pattern of seeing patterns where there are none is true throughout sports as well as Wall Street. In basketball, everyone knows players sometimes have "hot hands," games when they are on. Basketball players *feel it* when they are on a shooting streak. Fans see it. And behavioral economists and psychologists study it, only to find that streak shooting is merely an illusion, not supported by statistical reality.

The most famous analysis of whether or not certain basketball players have hot hands was conducted on the Philadelphia '76ers. Cornell psychologist Tom Gilovich asked members of the team about their own view of hot hands. The players reported knowing when they were going to make their next shot. If they had made many shots in a row, their feeling was they "almost couldn't miss the next one." They also passed the ball to a player who just made several shots in a row, because they agreed that player was "on" and less likely to miss.

The psychologists then examined the actual performance of the team's shooting record. To take some of the complicating factors out of the analysis, they looked at foul shots. Here no passing was involved, no selection of extra tough shots, no changes in defense to crush a hot player. Free throws allow you to look at player's skill at shooting in isolation.

And here is what Gilovich found: There were no streaks that were any better than statistical chance. The likelihood of making a second shot, based on a hit or a miss on the first shot, was not significantly different from zero. As Gilovich and his co-authors report, there "is no evidence the outcome of the second free throw is influenced by the outcome of the first free throw." This startling finding has been replicated again and again: with college undergraduate basketball players and with professional teams.

Gilovich looked at streakiness in other ways. He measured the actual success of players who "knew" they were going to make their next shot and observers who believed this, too. The players were largely unable to successfully predict a hit or a miss, and the observers were completely unable to predict it. All that was clear is where these predictions came from: if a player had hit or missed the previous shot. This explained whether a player felt "hot or not" but not if he was likely to make his next shot.

These findings are hard to handle. Part of our intuitive problem is events may look like a streak but in fact still be within the realms of pure chance. For instance, the outcome of heads or tails is roughly 50/50. Even so, you can still get heads four times in a row. In fact, this is *likely* to actually occur in 20 tosses, according to random chance. The odds of the next toss are unaffected. (See Chapter 21, "The Truth About Coin Tosses: They Aren't Fair," for more about secret biases in coin tosses.)

I spoke to Gilovich about his interpretation of his "hot hand" theory, which has been so important to the development of behavioral economics. He admitted that most people don't believe it. When he teaches his findings, *none* of his students ever believe it. I'm not sure *I* believe it.

"Part of the problem is you certainly feel you are in a flow state. That is a true feeling. But in basketball, that feeling, and past performance, doesn't predict future performance. Making several in a row doesn't predict you are going to make your next basket. The clustering of hits and misses is no different from the clustering you see when you are flipping coins."

Nonetheless, the belief that a player is hot or cold has consequences. Coaches keep players they believe are on a streak in the game longer. They may get passed the ball more often. Of course, differences in skill exist between players. Some hit or miss shots more often.

But Gilovich is only looking at streaks: If you made your last shot, is there a better chance you will make your next one? Says Gilovich, "This can be shown not to be the case."

For Gilovich, his work is really a metaphor for gambling...and stock market behavior. Wall Street traders strongly believe in hot streaks and cold streaks, too. When traders are "hot" the sense is their feelings are completely in sync with the market. Their bosses grab them, before they lose their hotness, and put them to work trading. Gilovich has a cooler view of this sort of phenomenon: "Gamblers feel they are on a roll, but we know this isn't true. The odds of getting three heads in a row is one out of eight. There is no streak if this occurs. But gamblers may feel it, and so do stock pickers." A company may have an unexpectedly positive earnings announcement. Then it has three in a row. The stock at this point spikes upward and seems unstoppable. The firm may be on a fantastic growth path. But it might not be. The outcome is not unexpected under the rules of chance, although the market doesn't acknowledge this. It may be time to bet against the stock.

17

Fourth and Ten: Insights into NFL (and Corporate) Decision Making

"Winning isn't everything, it's the only thing" legendary football coach Vince Lombardi said, according to legend. This sentiment may have been true of his Green Bay Packers, but does it describe most corporate behavior today? Does the strategy and track record of corporations show they are trying to do the best they can financially, to "win" at whatever game they are in?

Logically the answer would have to be yes—corporations are there to make money. Milton Friedman saw this as a nonissue, arguing, "Unless the behavior of businessmen in some way or other approximated behavior consistent with the maximization of returns, it seems unlikely that they would remain in business for long.... The process of 'natural selection' thus helps to validate the hypothesis."

It's hard to know if corporations really are trying to maximize profits or are just taking it easy. The whole industry may be taking the slow road. Detroit's "Big Three" automakers come to mind. Corporations' true strategic objectives are hard to identify, even with access to inside information. Even if you were there at that corporate strategic retreat with consultant-led thought exercises, whatever you overheard might not come to pass when it came time for implementation. Corporations are so large, and markets so quickly changing, that it is hard to clearly identify and disentangle a company's true strategic objectives.

This has led many economists back to...football. The choices football teams face on the field are similar to corporate strategic decisions—to go long, to punt, to try for the touchdown. Instead of being about maximizing returns or winning profits, the issue is simply about winning. The decisions are easier study than those of a corporation: The data is right there on the sports pages. And unlike academic decisions and experiments in a classroom, which are open to the criticism of not holding up in real life, in football the stakes are very high. It's for real.

David Romer is an economics professor at Berkeley who studies the starkest decision facing football teams: what to do on fourth down. Go for it, attempt a field goal, or punt? What should they do? What do they do?

Romer looked at fourth downs in 700 games. The nitty-gritty of his analysis is very rigorous, involving mathematical techniques such as "dynamic programming" and expected payoffs. His conclusions, though, are very simple and striking:

> "Teams' choices on fourth downs differ from the choices that would maximize their chances of winning in ways that are systematic and overwhelmingly statistically significant. Indeed, there are cases where teams consistently make choices that represent clear-cut and large departures from win-maximization."

The general gist is that teams are too risk averse on their fourth down decisions. Take for example, the situation of fourth and goal on the opponent's two-yard line early in the game. Romer's data shows that going for a touchdown has a 3/7th likelihood of succeeding. Going for the field goal has a near certainty of producing three points. Therefore, in terms of likely points scored, the decisions are in fact *equally* good (the calculation is 3/7 chance of getting a touchdown × 7 points for a touchdown = 3, which is the same number of points as a field goal.). But in terms of the opponent's field position that results from the play, the two couldn't be more different. A play that succeeds will lead to a kickoff, giving the opponent the chance of a good return. Going for the field goal will pretty much guarantee this. Going for the touchdown, in contrast, is a win/win. You have a 3/7th's chance of succeeding, but if you don't, the other team will only get the ball on the two-yard line.

Once you factor in the field position, the two plays are no longer comparable. The touchdown attempt has the edge. Romer calculates that going for the touchdown would increase the team's chance of winning by three percentage points because of the added benefit of great defensive field position in case of a failure. But when they were faced with this decision (that is, fourth and goal on the two-yard line, *every* team in his sample went for the field goal).

Even when they were on the one-yard line, teams played it safe. Romer found going for the touchdown on fourth and goal at the one-yard line, compared to the field goal, improved the odds of winning the game by 5%. But teams went for the touchdown about only half the time.

At midfield, if its fourth and one, Romer's statistics show that teams should go for the first down. The likelihood of a first down outweighs the bad field position that results from a failure. The precise breakpoint, according to Romer, is as follows: "On the team's own half of the field, going for it is better on average as long as there are less than about four yards to go." But this is not the conventional wisdom—statistically, teams in this situation prefer to play it safe and punt.

Romer's findings aren't controversial, at least not in economics, but this isn't true in the NFL. Romer is not a football player, not that I know of. (I do know that he is half of an all-star economics couple. His wife, Christina Romer, is chair of the Council of Economic Advisors for President Obama.) Although he admits his results about optimal versus actual football strategy were "surprising," he was more surprised by the reaction of NFL teams to his work. There *wasn't* any, although the findings were widely known and discussed in NFL circles. Romer seems miffed that when presented with new evidence

NFL coaches didn't seem that interested in pursuing, or at least testing, these unconventional ideas. Of course, teams aren't just sitting around waiting to try out a new anomaly unearthed by an academic economist, but this isn't always the case. They have been very open to new ideas about draft picks (see the next chapter).

Romer's assessment is that the lack of uptake by coaches has to do with the spirit of football itself. Teams prefer to think of the game as a long, drawn-out fair fight, a moral struggle, where the best team wins on merit rather than high-risk gambling strategies. Vince Lombardi was wrong: Winning isn't the only thing for football teams. Conventionality is important, too.

These strategic shortcomings are supported by psychology. Humans, including football coaches, are risk averse. Intuitively, not going for the first down *feels* safer. Romer says the reaction he gets from anyone who hears his ideas—for instance, his advice that you should go for it when you are fourth and one on the 50-yard line—is the same one: "People always say, 'If you fail that will be bad.' Not a single person has said, 'Wow, if you succeed that will be great.'" People put too much on weight on negative outcomes. Coaches and teams prefer to play it safe. But they only think they are because by doing so they are damaging their chance of winning.

This football analysis is really an analogy for corporate behavior. Romer's findings about football strategy, as well as teams' reactions to his finding, show that a competitive environment doesn't automatically lead to great decisions. Corporations—and investors—need to be open to the idea that organizations make systematic mistakes even in repeated high-stakes situations. They just may not be aware of it. Wall Street has erred in the risk-seeking direction, but other, stodgier industries might be playing it too safe, even if this only leads to failure in the long run.

Financial Planning and Football

Ironically, if football teams play it too safe on the field, off the field football players take way too many risks with their money. The typical football player's financial story after the NFL is a sad one. They have a phrase for it in the NFL: the "riches to rags" story.

Take as an example the life of Dallas Cowboy Clayton Holmes. He could serve as the poster child for life after the NFL. Holmes played in three Super Bowls for the Cowboys and used to drive a white Mercedes 560 SEC. Twelve years later he gets around on a red bicycle. He lives in a shack without running water or electricity in the front yard of his mother's trailer. Holmes has no money left from his time in the NFL, only the memories, and a song he wrote about it, "Lord, Where My Life Go?"

These stories, of sudden riches and then a sudden return to poverty, have a behavioral finance component. Football players have a uniquely short professional life—3.5 years on average—much less than in other sports. Because of this, they have little chance to learn from their financial mistakes. Investing isn't necessarily intuitive, but it can become so through trial and error. Footballs players can't make an investing error; they don't get a second chance the way baseball players do, with their long careers. If a baseball player makes a bad investment or gives everything to an untrustworthy financial advisor, having learned the hard way, he has plenty of years left to replenish his portfolio. The average football player may earn three to four million dollars, but only within a very short window. And they have to find ways to make it last a lifetime.

The NFL Players Association (the players' union) is concerned about stories such as Clayton Holmes' and now teaches financial planning to players. The union's department for financial programs and education is run by Dana Hammonds. I caught up with her as she was returning from giving a presentation to the Professional Football Players Mothers' Association. The point of her presentation was to explain to the mothers that while the average corporate salary rises over time, the average football players' salary starts high but then plummets to zero within a few years. Players have to save during the good years. The message contained a painful truth. The mothers were beneficiaries of new homes and cars during these years. "Maybe they shouldn't have accepted the gifts," Dana told the mothers. "Maybe they should have just said 'no.'"

"How did they react to this message?" I asked. Dana's response: "They loved it."

Dana teaches the players a similar story, as well as financial basics such as what is a stock, what is a bond. She also teaches budgeting. Players only get paid for 17 weeks and have to make this last a year. Hammonds call this "their sure money," and they have to make it last. Players also have "if" money—if they make the playoffs, if they go to the Super Bowl. Hammonds tells players they need to distinguish between the "sure" money and the "if" money.

Her main focus is psychological. As she explained to me, "Most players are coming into sudden money. They need to understand their relationship and experiences and their past with money. Now is the time to develop a more healthy relationship with money." Healthy means not buying expensive toys—or friendships. This will render them broke when their career is over. The main message, once the players understand the basics of investing, is not to be impulsive. The association counsels self-control when it comes to money. Dana says, "We tell them 'Your career is based on only 3.5 years. There probably won't be another time when you make this money, so don't take risks.' Basically, we try to get them to understand if they have better self-control, the chances they will become victims of fraud will be greatly limited and the money will last."

18

Football Stories, Continued: The NFL Draft

In the 1998 NFL football draft, the focus was on the two top prospects, both star college quarterbacks—Ryan Leaf and Peyton Manning. Leaf, who was going pro immediately after an impressive season as a college junior, was considered to have the stronger arm. Manning, son of illustrious quarterback Archie Manning, was seen as the overall better player. It wasn't clear who was going to be the top draft choice. Instead, the differences between the two top players were seen as so small that the real battle would be who would be able to get them. Manning ended up as draft pick #1 and went to the Colts. Leaf was #1A and went to the San Diego Chargers. The Chargers went to considerable effort to draft him, trading two first-round picks to do so, and guaranteeing Leaf an $11.25-million signing bonus, the largest ever for a rookie at that time.

But the trajectory of the two quarterbacks' subsequent careers was not as evenly matched, as might have been predicted from the draft. Manning went on to be the only player in NFL history to pass 4,000 yards in five consecutive seasons. Leaf went on to be one of the biggest flops in NFL history. He was quickly released by the Chargers and retired at age 26. Leaf is currently a golf coach at West Texas A&M.

As the Manning-versus-Leaf draft shows, rank in the NFL draft reflects past performance. But it is not a perfect indicator of future performance. A huge amount of uncertainty is involved. How good are teams and their scouts at differentiating stars from flops? How valuable is a star compared to a lesser player? Another set of questions is, How good do scouts *think* they are? And how good can they ever be?

The Chart

To assist them in these efforts, NFL organizations use something they call "the chart" to assess the fair value for trading draft picks. It is a mathematical table with each pick assigned a point value. The computations involved are complex: One early-round draft pick—who on average costs more—can be traded for multiple later-round picks. The chart, according to NFL lore, was invented by a business partner of Dallas Cowboys' head coach Jimmy Johnson. Johnson used it to statistically outmaneuver rivals as he created the legendary Cowboys of the 80s and 90s. The methodology behind the chart leaked out to other teams, and now the whole league is believed to use versions of the chart to value trades and draft picks.

Star football players, according the chart, are worth more—a huge amount more—than ordinary players. The typical chart shows a drop-off in value within the first round of the draft, and then a steep drop-off as the draft goes into later rounds. Even within the first round of the draft, the top picks are calculated as being worth four times the later players. And later-round picks command only a relative pittance.

The chart only indicates the market value of the right to choose, say, the tenth or twentieth draft choice. The draft order itself, of each individual player, comes out of the NFL Scouting Combine held in Indianapolis each year. Only the top prospects are invited, to spend a week going through test after test in front of NFL couches, scouts, general managers, and trainers. The players allegedly even parade around in their underwear so scouts can see their musculature and definition. The tests are primarily physical: 40-yard dash, broad jump, bench press—how many times a player can bench press 225 pounds;

quarterbacks and wide receivers are exempted from this. Players also have to undergo a mental test, the Wonderlic, which was originally developed for use by corporate "personnel departments" in the 1930s.

The use of the chart, the week spent at the combine, and the presence of scouts and agents—to say nothing of the huge amount of money involved—all show that the NFL draft is a far from naive process. It isn't akin to a lone daytrader sitting at home trying to pick the next Microsoft. It's more like an investment bank's (or several investment banks') vast research department trying to analyze a complex mortgage-backed security. This analogy isn't far off: Despite the sophistication of those involved, as the Leaf-versus-Manning draft shows, sometimes the process falls apart.

The NFL draft has attracted the attention of two behavioral economists: Cade Massey of Yale working with Richard Thaler of the University of Chicago. They undertook their own analysis of the complex draft choices facing NFL teams. As part of their analysis, they compared the market value of draft picks to their later on-field performance. Their overall conclusion: "Teams overestimated their ability to discriminate between stars and flops."

In particular, the performance differences between two players ranked adjacently in the draft were essentially unpredictable, even though scouts insist otherwise. Beyond this, analyzing the performance (and salaries) of early-round draft picks compared to picks from the late rounds showed that both performance and pay drifted down for the later picks, as both intuition and "the chart" would predict. But the chart had too negative of a view: Some of the later picks were effectively undervalued at their price. This is also reflected in the small amount of time scouts spent on them, with virtually all attention focused on the first-round picks.

A central, and perhaps more surprising failure of the NFL draft is, "high draft-picks are bad investments," as the two economists write. Take, for example, the performance of running backs and wide receivers within the first round. The top picks were indeed the top performers, but they weren't worth it at the price. Their results on the field weren't commensurate with their star salaries. The "yards gained per dollar of compensation" (an unusual but revealing football stat) was better for players deeper in round one of the draft or the top of the second round, compared to the superstars. Given salary caps in football (another extremely complex subject), buying top stars regardless of the cost doesn't pay off. Instead, teams could have improved their performance by swapping away the rights to a first-round pick for several second-round picks.

Massey, as an economist, is focused on market values that arise from "the chart" rather than individual performance as judged at the combine. But as he points out, "The Wonderlic psychological test has never been validated for football that I know of. But then again neither have 40-yard-dash times." Scouts may be overweighting, or underweighting, certain physical attributes; Massey simply hasn't studied these—yet.

However, he is not an armchair economist. Massey doesn't just study old data from NFL drafts; he and Thaler consult for an NFL franchise (they won't say which one), sharing their behavioral insights. The big finding—that teams were effectively overpaying for the star top pick—was initially seen as complete blasphemy. The team is now open to this idea, but as Massey admits, "It is really hard for people to change the way they go about this. There is a culture. A history. The way things are done. It is hard for people to let go of that." It flies in the face of intuition and what scouts are paid to do.

There may be something inherent in the draft, or really in any similar bidding process, that causes people to overvalue what they think of as "the best." In football, the problem may be that teams and scouts "fall in love" with certain prospects. Even though Massey and Thaler have 10,000 observations they can share with a team, this objectivity flies out the window when a scout is smitten with a player and loses objectivity.

The team has put into place some practical solutions based on Massey's and Thaler's insights. One is to *not* personalize the potential picks. The scout whose job is to value trades and manage the teams "portfolio" of picks, now makes a point of not learning anything about a college player before the draft, aside from statistical information. He feels this makes him more objective. The scout also doesn't become overwhelmed with irrelevant information that might improve his confidence about his draft choices—but not his accuracy.

It's Only Business...

One obvious analogue of the NFL draft case study is hiring decisions. Fleeting but strong first impressions from a short job interview may outweigh more objective criteria. The manager gets over-involved in the heat of the moment, just like a football scout falling in love with a pick, and forgets the bigger picture. Psychologist refer to this as "case-based" decision making. It's hard get beyond the case and step outside your emotions to incorporate larger, more impersonal information in your reasoning.

The real problem isn't picking the best; it's admitting that you are really choosing between two similar gambles, but gambles nonetheless. And the future is unknowable, unless you want to hire them both. Cade Massey interprets his results to me this way: "There is no crime in not being able to identify the best hire; the crime is not being able to admit it. The solution is to have a healthy appreciation of uncertainty."

The NFL chart lesson doesn't just hold for picking employees or football players—it's true for choosing investment funds as well. The erratic performance of money managers, such as hedge funds or mutual funds, after being hired (or fired) by pension plans, is a case in point. These managers are selected based on extensive quantitative and qualitative evaluation by sophisticated pension consultants. The whole enterprise of selecting the best institutional money managers is fraught with uncertainty with little to show for all the effort involved. It's actually worse than this: Pension plans make terrible hiring decisions in terms of deciding which hedge fund or mutual funds gets a piece of their investments.

Once the hot new money manager has been hired by the pension plan, he or she almost immediately stumbles. "Post-hiring returns are statistically indistinguishable from zero," according to Amit Goyal and Sunil Wahal, two academics who study the hiring and firing of money managers. In contrast, managers who have been fired by the plan often suddenly do much better, and start beating the market. In short, hired managers experience a drop-off in performance, and fired managers typically rebound. The hiring process by pension plans seems to get it exactly wrong.

Essentially, the pension funds and their consultants are chasing returns, believing that past performance predicts future performance. The opposite appears to be the case. Simple mean reversion has more predictive power than any complex algorithm. In this case, *not* hiring new managers (and not firing the old ones) is the way to go.

19

The Inner Game of Tennis, Revisited

The 1970s bestseller *The Inner Game of Tennis,* by Timothy Gallwey, provided a method for overcoming psychological hang-ups when it comes to tennis (and life). Gallwey observed that most players are unable to reach their full potential because they are tripped up by their inner mental game, which is characterized by self-consciousness and self-condemnation. In essence, players over-think, overriding their natural physical talents. Gallwey, who was well versed in Zen philosophy and the overall 1970s zeitgeist, provided actual solutions to these problems. His central advice was "Let it happen." Players could free themselves to play their best by quieting their mind and not getting distracted by conscious thinking. Get into the "zone." (Another self-help guru popularized this term, not Gallwey, but it's the same idea.)

Inner Game swept the tennis world, helped in part by an accompanying PBS mini-series as well as by fans such as Billie Jean King. The insights then spread to golf ("the inner game of golf") skiing, music, and now corporate America. The message remains the same: Trust the mind/body connection and you will be free to perform at your best.

When it comes to tennis, the real rationale for playing the inner game is to prevent choking. Malcolm Gladwell describes choking this way: "It is about thinking too much. Choking is about loss of instinct." He uses the concept to dissect the failure of the Czech star Jana Novotna to defeat Steffi Graff in the Wimbledon Finals in 1993.

Novotna was up 4-1 in the second set, having already won the first. As victory came within reach, Gladwell describes what happened next: "Jana Novotna faltered—she began thinking about her shots again. She lost her fluidity, her touch. She double-faulted on her serves and mis-hit her overheads, the shots that demand the greatest sensitivity in force and timing." Novotna ultimately lost the set and the match and collapsed into tears at the awards ceremony.

The concept of the inner game makes sense when it comes to tennis. Because tennis involves physical action, you usually want to rely upon your quick intuitive system, rather than forcing your slower analytical thinking system to call the shots.

But analytical thinking may still be useful for some of the shots. Tennis also involves strategy. Choking may be an issue for some players, but the very top players are facing something more challenging: highly skilled opponents. Their intuition has to work out complex strategies and the probabilities of different shots against rivals who are not likely to make unforced errors. And we know that when it comes to math—and probabilities in particular—our intuition rarely produces superb results.

The Dutch econometrician Jan Magnus has examined the strategy of the top-ranked players at Wimbledon, to try and decipher their tactics and the probabilities of winning different shots to see if in fact there is room for improvement. His focus is on the serve. Tennis players can either serve "hard" or "softer," with varying degrees of difficulty for an opponent. For a hard serve, the probability of winning a point is higher, but so is the likelihood of a service fault. An easier serve means there is a higher probability the ball will go in, but the overall probability of winning the point is lowered.

For Magnus, this becomes a math problem. His work involves 20 pages or so of difficult probability calculations, plus data to work out the potential tradeoff between hard and softer serves. But the key insight, or rather question, is simple: Do the very top players instinctively hit upon what is the mathematically correct service strategy? The answer is no.

They certainly do it better than mere mortals, but they still depart from perfection. Their weak spot is figuring out how hard to hit the second serve. Boris Becker, once nicknamed "Boom Boom" because of his powerful service, encountered this problem when facing Pete Sampras at Wimbledon in 1995. Sampras had a powerful return, so Becker used a powerful second serve. But he overdid it, and began over-hitting the second serve. The result is he double-faulted 15 times.

Becker was back at Wimbledon four years later, against Patrick Rafter, but this time he began under-hitting his serves. He said in an interview at the time, "I tried to take something off the first serve and play it safely, but he started to return incredibly. It was a struggle." Becker lost in straight sets.

Magnus's complicated mathematical calculations are exactly that—too complicated for the brain to process immediately. Instead, people have to approximate the results, using "simplified" (Magnus won't say "dumbed-down") rules of thumb. The top players do a pretty good job of it. Maybe they have better inner games and fewer of the emotional hurdles of everyone else. But this still doesn't mean they are perfect and perhaps could benefit from Magnus insights.

Magnus is an athlete, but professionally he's as an economist, and to him it is within this realm where the importance of this tennis lesson lies. Wimbledon can be viewed as a giant economics experiment. Players have to make choices among different strategies, with different risks involved. Big sums of money are at stake. Even the best players aren't perfect. And further down in the rankings, Magnus has found the strategies of these players are much worse.

The outcome of this experiment holds meaning for corporate strategy. Even the best companies are probably not making perfect strategic decisions compared to what they could be doing. And companies further behind are probably even more off target. Corporations, even the best, are therefore far from optimal, or even rational in their strategies, according to this analysis.

But these econometric findings are also interesting for tennis. They offer new ideas of how players can improve the strategy in their own game. The easiest area to fix is in returns. (Targeting the precise hardness on the first or second serve is more of an issue for pros, who are pretty good at this anyway, just not perfect.)

Statistically, the server has a huge advantage. The receiver in tennis is likely, even expected, to lose. If you just play it safe as a receiver, you are almost guaranteed to lose, given your strategic disadvantages compared to the server. Therefore, it pays to take risks. Be erratic; try to go for high-payoff low-probability shots. It doesn't matter if you are likely to lose anyway. Your objective is to just break serve once in a while. In particular, Magnus's recommendation is to try to hit return shots close to the line.

You can still get in touch with your inner game on each shot and remain relaxed. But it helps to understand the overall odds of a specific situation. If the odds are in your favor, you can afford to play it safe. But if the odds are against you, such as when you are receiving in tennis from a better player, you have to take more risks. Sounding every bit like the sports or corporate guru he of course isn't, Magnus's conclusion for tennis and life is, "Playing it safe is not always a safe strategy."

20

How to Make Money Gambling: Behavioral Insights

How do you make money gambling? You own the casino...so goes the old Vegas joke.

The founding fathers of Las Vegas, that is, gangsters, were psychologically sophisticated when it came to understanding gamblers. Given that odds are always in favor in the house and against the gambler, the trick was to find ways to sell the customer what, on the face of it, was a losing proposition. The marketing strategies the early casino bosses came up with were unparalleled in corporate America, a tradition that continues to this day, albeit in a contemporary form.

The Psychology of Design and Las Vegas

The centerpiece of these early strategies involved making a loser *feel* like a winner. Casino architect Alan Lapidus (son of Miami Beach architect Morris Lapidus) gives a glimpse of this process in his book *Everything by Design.* To take an example from 1950s Vegas, suppose a gambler is already down $40,000. His credit limit is only $50,000. The pit boss, seeing the gambler approaching his credit limit, steps in. He suggests the client give the dice a break; maybe catch the show while letting them "warm up." Lapidus quotes an old timer who explains what happens next to the gambler:

"He goes to the night club and...the maitre d' ushers him to a ringside table. There is a bottle of Dom Perignon cooling in an ice bucket, a box of Havanas are sitting on the table, and a bunch of topless cuties are shaking it in his face. A little while later the maitre d' asks which of them he'd like. He has a night to remember."

To complete the process, the next morning the casino gives the gambler a free car, a Cadillac convertible (bought at a discount). The casino is up $40,000 minus the cost of the car and salaries, but the gambler is up, too. To use a technical term from psychology, the casino had successfully "reframed" the encounter, making the loser appear to himself to be a winner.

This psychological astuteness touches every area of casino life, including architecture and layout. Lapidus says the interior environment of the casino is carefully thought out: "Nothing [is] by chance, everything by design." As is immediately obvious to every visitor, there are no clocks in the casino, no daylight and sunset, no outside world. In short, no time at all...like the present. Guests in Vegas have to cross the gaming floor to go anywhere. The slot machines are kept on the edge, as a lure, and a place for gamblers to deposit loose change. Table games, such as Blackjack, are in the middle. At the center is the Baccarat pit, the most exclusive area, designated for high rollers—and high profits for the casino.

The constant focus on psychology includes even the cocktail waitress costumes. Casinos recognized clients might find the women intimidating as *individuals*. The solution was to make them generic fantasy figures by providing them with uniform headdresses and wigs. Lapidus terms these and similar efforts "exercises in applied psychology."

Casino expertise in the psychology of design could interest behavioral policymakers. The newest area of behavioral finance policy research is focused on the "architecture of choice." In this approach, policymakers alter the context of choices, how they are framed or displayed, to significantly improve decisions and outcomes. There is no need to change economic incentives. In their book *Nudge,* academics and choice architects Richard Thaler and Cass Sunstein use school cafeterias as an example. Simply by moving around the display of foods, spotlighting fruits and vegetables and keeping junk food largely out of sight and therefore out of mind, the cafeteria director could increase the consumption of healthy foods. Thaler and Sunstein extend this hypothetical cafeteria example to other areas of life, such as 401(k) plans, health insurance, and Social Security. In each case, the design of choices can "nudge" people in the right direction.

Casino people such as Lapidus are already well aware of the power of "choice architecture." Their results aren't hypothetical, making them an untapped resource in how to expertly design physical environments that affect choices. Of course, policymakers are presumably charged with using nudges to *improve* the lives of others. However, they may have a hard time relying upon insights from the Strip or turning for counsel to casino designers as the elder statesmen of choice architecture.

Harrah's

The largely intuitive marketing efforts of historical Vegas were appropriate when gambling was a lightly regulated, cottage industry. The free cars and more were targeted in any case only to high rollers. But in today's corporate casino world, with gaming now a major mass-market draw conducted in numerous states across the U.S., new approaches are called for. The challenge remains the same: The primary economic incentives facing the client—their odds of winning—are not in their favor. Changing the payouts on slots is not legal or desirable. Casino's have to find ways to appeal to client's hopes rather than their rational economic calculations or enlightened self-interest, either of which could put a damper on gambling.

Gary Loveman, CEO of Harrah's, the world's largest gaming company, is an economist by training; he has a Ph.D. from MIT. He was a professor at Harvard Business School when he was recruited by Harrah's.

His approach to marketing is unprecedented in gambling, and maybe other businesses as well. He scientifically models and tests consumer behavior, drawing upon econometrics, epidemiological methods, and, yes, behavioral economics.

Speaking from Atlantic City, a major Harrah's outpost, Loveman explained to me how he transformed casino marketing. Whereas the industry founders just relied on their gut instincts, Loveman refines and tests all insights, making marketing more of a science and one rooted in a precise understanding of consumer behavior and psychology.

Interestingly, he begins our conversation by talking about love, corporate love: "If somebody loves you, it's because they feel great about you as brand. You don't have to use discounting." Financial incentives alone are not the way to make consumers fall in love with a particular company, which is obvious to anyone but an economist. You can't buy love. Instead, Loveman suggests corporations should continuously monitor consumer behavior and in some cases modify it, to make sure customers fall in love with the brand. "And in this area," says Loveman, "we are as strategic and surgical as we can be."

Loveman's bet upon arriving at Harrah's was to focus on improving revenues from existing facilities, analogous to pursuing a same-store-sales growth strategy used in retail. Most of his competitors instead were adding to their facilities, making them glossier—putting in exploding volcano displays—and bigger, with most revenue growth coming from an expanding gambling floor. But Harrah's already had geographically diversified facilities, and, in fact, was soon to become the largest gambling operation in the world.

Loveman immediately set about improving customer service. When he started, he found something else: Harrah's had a sort of rudimentary customer rewards program, giving out points for gambling, akin to an airline's frequent-flier program. Loveman had no interest in the effectiveness of the program as it was then designed—it had none. But the program did allow the casino to collect extensive information on customer preferences, even if the casino didn't know what to do with this information. Loveman, as a social scientist, immediately recognized he had a rich data set at his disposal. He could put it to use in a way no other casino boss could envision. It is his interpretation and exploitation of the customer preference data to hone his marketing strategy that sets Harrah's apart.

"Take a basic example," says Loveman. "When we first started, I found we were giving customers from Chicago a discounted room and beverage in Vegas as well as a $35 dollar gift certificate for the gift shop. We found that the gift certificate was not predictive of a trip, but was used if people came." In other words, the gift certificate brought in no customers, but customers who did come spent the $35, an instant loss for the casino. The gift certificate was not fulfilling any of the casino's marketing objectives and was just a dead loss. Loveman instead found that reducing the room rate was more likely to spur traveling to Vegas—that was a clear fact from his data. "Simply by decreasing the room rate by $15 dollars, we were able to increase the response rate. And when they came, the trip was more profitable for us."

"Take a more complex example," continues Loveman, in a slightly pedagogical mode that harkens back to college teaching: "Let's imagine a woman of 61 years of age in suburban Memphis drives to our casino in Tunica, Mississippi, for the first time, plays a $10 slot once, and leaves." Under historical gaming marketing analysis, she would have all the signs of being a lousy customer. She, after all, spent only $10 dollars. The casino might try sending her a free buffet coupon, but probably would do nothing at all. However, Loveman's complex model would reach different conclusions. It turns out being 61, and from suburban Memphis, are both good things when it comes to gambling. And she played a $10 slot machine rather than something smaller, indicative of a higher roller.

"Using our predictive model, we would predict her gambling budget is substantial. In fact, she is likely playing at a competitor's. The only way to market to her meaningfully is to market to her competitively," says Loveman. In her case, this might mean a free room, or possibly a suite, and show tickets. There are many amenities Loveman could try. But at the same time the model's hypothesis might be wrong. The 61-year-old might not be such a great prospect. Free parking alone might do the job of luring her back.

The key point is Harrah's *tests* its marketing hypothesis every week. The casino observes the behavior of thousands of gamblers, like the hypothetical visitor from Memphis. For testing purposes, they are placed into active and control groups. The active group gets different marketing from the control group say, a suite. The control group gets something more modest, such as free parking. The casino then analyzes the difference. Loveman and team decide whether they learned anything, and if they did, they get the message out to 50 other facilities, and then move on to the next test.

Harrah's still makes use of traditional Vegas-oriented service approaches. Slot machine players can leave their machines untouched if they want while they go to dinner or a show and then return to a machine no one else has played. The casino caters to many gambling folk beliefs. But what it can't do is change the odds, except on a very few high-end games for high-end gamblers.

If Harrah's is at the leading edge of moving away from intuition to a more rigorous assessment of consumer behavior, with all its seemingly idiosyncratic but largely predictable responses, who is at the lagging edge? Tired of all the positive news, I wanted something negative, so I asked Loveman, "Who *doesn't* get it?" Here is his response:

> "Grocery stores do the worst job of any organizations I've seen. They do just about everything wrong. They do it backwards. If you are coming to see me in St. Louis every Saturday night, the last thing I want to do is discount the Saturday night trip."

But that is exactly what grocery stores mistakenly do, he argues. If you buy a lot of diapers, grocery stores give you a discount on diapers.

Instead, they should give you a coupon for a product you don't buy. Loveman recommends "a high margin product, like skin cream."

His more "out of the box" suggestion is to change the way grocery store lines are organized. Currently, express lines are only available for customers who have bought just a few things. If you have a full cart, though, you have to wait in a long line. This means, as Loveman points out, grocery stores reward people who spend the least with the best lines, whereas people spending the most have the worst lines. "Your best customers should come first in service satisfaction, not last," he says, and be given the fastest lines.

This is a suggestion too far for me. I've spent enough time trapped in airport check-in lines, while first-class passengers whisk by and through security as well. (Why are they lower security risks?) Simple fairness as well as expediency counteract the corporate revenue-maximizing perspective inherent in Loveman's idea. But even if it is misguided, it is imaginative.

This candor extends to his description of an additional aspect of his constant testing: the testing is "symmetrical." That is, whereas some tests try to determine where the casino should increase financial incentives, other tests try to find out where the casino could *reduce* financial incentives. The analysis cuts both ways. High frequency gamblers, flying in from Chicago to Vegas, could be induced to visit with a $100 coupon. However, $75 might also do the trick. Time for a test to find out. Says Loveman, "If we can get the number weaned down that doesn't impact frequency, getting them to come and stay for less money, then that is powerful learning, too."

Las Vegas is distinctive. The way high-end customers are treated is unique. Marketing to them is very "involved," a euphemism encompassing any number of methods, from free shows, to diamond watches as gifts, and more. But marketing to the masses, at least in Harrah's case, is now unique as well.

Behavioral economics can be deployed in new ways—ways that maximize corporate revenues but minimize customer assets. Not every intervention is a win-win, certainly not in Las Vegas. But there is an honesty about the stakes involved, an honesty missing from the gaming industry's close cousin: Wall Street. The lessons may be dark ones, but in economics as in many areas of life, we have much to learn from Las Vegas.

21

The Truth About Coin Tosses:
They Aren't Fair

Heads or tails. How to call it? Do you think it's random, unpredictable? We use coin tosses to settle disputes and decide outcomes, because we believe they are unbiased with 50/50 odds. And we use them metaphorically, too. "It's a coin toss" means something could go either way.

Our bias is that coin tosses are fair. But they aren't—they have a bias. The odds are not 50/50 heads/tails. Instead, a tossed coin tends to come up the same side as it started. Heads facing up predicts heads; tails facing up predicts tails. So much for our intuition. The statistical differences involved are too subtle for us to notice, but they are real nonetheless. Three academics—Persi Diaconis, Susan Holmes, and Richard Montgomery—through vigorous analysis made this small but interesting discovery. As they write in their published results, "Dynamical Bias in the Coin Toss":

> "For natural flips, the chance of coming up as started is about 51%."

The reason why coin tosses aren't random has to do with the laws of mechanics. As the academics note, "their flight is determined by their initial conditions." Susan Holmes, a statistician at Stanford, told me most people when hearing about this weird finding think it has something to do with the density of the coin, but she was able to disprove this by constructing a coin made out of balsa wood on one face and metal on the other. This made no difference to the flips. The dynamics of the coin flip, and its outcome, aren't determined by the lack of balance in the coin.

To understand more about flips, the academics built a coin-tossing machine and filmed it using a slow motion camera. This confirmed that the outcome of flips isn't random. It did show that the rotation of a flipping coin occurs around several different axes. Coins when tossed flip over and over, but they also spin around and around like pizza dough being twirled.

The laws of physics, rather than chance, determine the outcome of a flip. If the force of the flip is the same, the outcome is the same. The machine could make the toss come out heads every time. When people, rather than a machine, flipped the coin, there was still a slight physical bias favoring the position the coin started in. If the coin started heads up, then it would land heads up 51% of the time.

The true laws of coin tosses show yet again the inadequacy of our intuition—and perception—in even the most routine areas of life, and are central to gambling. I asked Holmes if coin flips used for, say, football, should be eliminated because they are biased. She pointed out that there is no reason to change the way the coin flip is done, as long as the person calling the flip doesn't know how the coin is going to start out. In football, the tosser is never the caller; the tosser is supposed to be a referee. But if you are both the caller and the tosser...well, that changes things. Knowing about the bias in coin tosses give you an edge, albeit a tiny one.

Holmes admits she still uses the metaphor of a coin toss in her statistics class at Stanford all the time—after all, the randomness in a coin toss is only very, very slightly off, with odds being 51/49. But certain people, when they flip a coin, can make it come out heads (or tails) 100% of the time. Persi Diaconis, Holmes' co-author and husband, is one of the people with this amazing talent. Before becoming a mathematician, he was a professional magician. Among his proofs is that it requires a full seven shuffles to truly randomize a deck of cards. He was admitted to graduate school at Harvard after two of his card tricks were published in *Scientific American*. So how exactly is Diaconis able to make a coin toss come out a certain way? Susan Holmes won't tell me: "It comes from his previous career—it's magic."

Part III
Personal Decisions: Personal Safety, Personal Finance, and Health Choices

Outside of financial markets or other quantitative situations, intuition can be immensely useful. This is most true in situations with evolutionary precedent that your intuition was designed for. Take, for instance, your personal life. Do you love your spouse? Your intuition knows for sure. Ruminating over this won't get you anywhere, and may only confuse you. Analytically, it doesn't mean you should leave him or her—after all, there are the children, the beach house, the 401(k) plan to consider—but in terms of basic love, your intuition knows the truth.

Physical danger is the classic example of where you have to listen to your instincts. Take the risk of avalanches. Mountain guides report intuitively knowing when an avalanche is about to occur. They can read all the avalanche reports they want, but if the snow doesn't look right, they won't go skiing on the mountain. The same is true for dangers posed by people. If you are walking down a dark alley and you get a "bad feeling," and the hair on the back of your neck starts standing up, your intuition is trying to tell you something it was designed for.

Malcolm Gladwell's *Blink* is an entire book chronicling the wonders of snap judgment, decisions that occur in just the blink of an eye, compared to slower more conscious deliberations. In just one of his many stories demonstrating the power of a glance, he discusses the dilemma facing Getty Museum antiquities curator Marion True. She

was considering acquiring a rare Greek statue that was in such remark-
able shape that it was a truly extraordinary find. Or was it a fake? Rather
than trusting her gut, she hired a geologist to analyze the statue's com-
position using an electron microscope and other high-tech instruments.
It passed the test. The Getty, led by True, decided to go ahead with the
$10-million purchase.

But before the museum wrote the check, the Getty held a sympo-
sium to continue debating the purchase. New advisors simply *looked*
at the statue—and they immediately *saw* a problem. The statue
looked "fresh," meaning not ancient. The group had an "intuitive
repulsion" about the statue. And further analysis supported this intuition, revealing the statue was, in fact, a fake. The earlier, supposedly
objective analysis was proven to be false. Intuition and snap judgments revealed more about the authenticity of the statue than more
careful analysis. Marion True, after her near debacle, learned to trust
her gut: "I always considered scientific opinion more objective than
aesthetic judgments," Gladwell reports her as saying. "Now I realize I
was wrong."

But sometimes more careful analysis is critical. Following the
publication of *Blink*, Marion True resurfaced again in the media, for
another decision. Having become a convert to the power of first
impressions, of thinking without thinking, the antiquities curator
encountered a new problem: She is currently on trial in Italy for ille-
gally trafficking in stolen antiquities. Specifically, True is alleged to
have been involved in a criminal conspiracy to loot Italian art objects
and also to be in receipt of stolen property. The Italian case has been
going on since 2005 and could go on for many more years. If con-
victed, True faces time in jail. Of course, nothing has been proven
against her, but Marion True is no longer affiliated with Getty. True's
L.A.-based attorney, Harry Stang, said to me, "She is innocent of the
charges and intends to fully defend them."

True may have been right to trust her first impressions to judge the authenticity of a statue, but legal statutes are not intuitive. You can't interpret Italian law with just the power of a glance. Rather than worrying so much whether or not a statue looked "fresh," maybe she and the Getty should have focused more on whether it was "hot." To be fair to True, everything she stands accused of was standard industry practice in the murky world of antiquities, a field she was actively trying to clean up. Her psychological error may have been to over-generalize from her experiences, to start intuiting what would permissible or not permissible to Italian authorities, and not appropriately recalibrate to a new and different prosecutorial environment.

What happened to Marion True after *Blink* should serve as a cautionary tale of relying too much on intuition. In the following chapters, I look at where intuition works and (mostly) doesn't work when it comes to some important personal decisions. I start with physical security. It turns out relying on your intuition to understand the physical threat someone poses to you is a surprisingly mixed bag; sometimes analytical thinking is more useful. I follow this with two chapters about personal finance—on credit cards and Social Security. Card issuers exploit the way we think and behave, but behavioral economics suggests a way to turn the tables. This is followed by a chapter on Social Security decisions; the best age to claim it is perhaps the most important financial decision of your life and one most people don't fully think through. The final chapters look at our intuition when it comes to healthcare decisions, from the way we interpret a diagnosis and guess the odds of surviving a disease, to how we choose health insurance. This part of the book concludes with an examination of intuitive mistakes we make while driving, revealing the true cause of many car accidents.

22

Personal Security: Assessing Danger

To learn about how adept our gut instincts are at sensing physical danger, I spoke to a former Secret Service agent about his experiences. Agent Joseph A. (J.A.) LaSorsa had been a member of Ronald Reagan's security detail when he was campaigning for President in 1980. J.A. LaSorsa now runs a security consulting and investigative firm in addition to providing an "executive protection training program," providing bodyguards for a worldwide booming security industry. I met with him in his South Florida office, which was secured behind locked doors and blacked-out windows.

LaSorsa told me a dramatic story of how he used his intuition in the field. Once he was guarding Reagan during a gathering of a small, hand-picked group of supporters in a meeting hall in New England. A young man wearing a parka, with his hands firmly in the pockets, walked up to Reagan. Agent LaSorsa kept an eye on the people in the room and the young man. The young man smiled as he stood there observing Reagan, but then the smile disappeared. He stared at the candidate and his face became cold, with his hands still in his pocket.

LaSorsa communicated to another agent that he was going to move in. Before the young man fully realized what was going on, LaSorsa grabbed him, placed his hands on the subject's coat pockets, and squeezed the contents of the pockets. It turns out the young supporter was clutching...a knit hat. It was a false alarm. The young man posed no threat. Looking back, did LaSorsa still think he did the right thing at that meeting room? "Yes, of course," he told me. "When you are in the field, you have to rely on what I call a sixth sense, a gut feeling that something bad might happen. If you are facing a possible event that might occur in the next five minutes, you don't have time to wait."

Yet this intuitive method is only part of the story when it comes to personal security. The Secret Service, when conducting a threat assessment of a potentially dangerous person, follows a systematic and analytical process. When training his students, LaSorsa teaches them formal techniques for evaluating a threat. The first step is to determine the "person of interest's" criminal history and mental history. The next step is to conduct background interviews with friends and neighbors. According to J.A., "If someone is spending all day alone in their basement skinning squirrels, well, that tells you something."

After looking into the threat's background and interviewing neighbors and family members about recent activities, the security expert's next step is to find out if the threat has any access to weapons. LaSorsa usually attempts a one-on-one interview with the potential-threat subject. The objective is to see if the person is capable of following through with a plan of action.

I asked LaSorsa where intuition comes into this process. "Um, it doesn't completely. You classify an individual as a serious threat, a benign threat, or no threat. You develop an opinion based on a workup, and you validate using either a gut feeling or empirical data, such as their past history. I usually go with the empirical."

J.A. LaSorsa destroyed my crisp argument that physical danger is always best judged by gut instincts. After all, there is an evolutionary precedent for threats from other humans, and our intuition evolved to quickly identify risks. LaSorsa, who seems like a nice guy, tried to accommodate my argument, to at least meet me halfway: He agreed that once you are out in the field you had to rely on your intuition. But when planning security, for the President or a South American socialite, a protection agent needs to rely upon a more analytical framework encompassing empirical facts and deliberately thought-out strategies.

Becoming overly analytical can create problems as well. As LaSorsa told me, "There is no quantitative matrix to give you a danger probability. Otherwise, the secret service would be using it. Nor is there too much room for a sixth sense. Instead, you have to rely primarily on empirical facts, and your personal experience of knowing what to look for."

If anything, executive protection and bodyguard work sounds strangely akin to investing, requiring a combination of quick but more often complex thinking.

23

Credit Card Stories: Beating Your Credit Card Charges Using Behavioral Economics

Please do something about this "legal loan sharking" that is going on. I ended up having to file bankruptcy a few years ago, thereby ruining my credit, because [my] Credit Card [company] decided to jack up my rates and everyone else followed suit. There was no clear indication of the reason for this action on their part as to why they raised my rates, since I was paying over the minimum on all my cards each month and was never late with a payment. Then right after I filed bankruptcy the credit card companies persuaded the government to change the bankruptcy laws...thereby pushing people's backs to the wall.

—Ron Sugg

My checks are sent in by the due date yet I continue to be charged late charges. I have looked at the deposit date on my check and it is several days later than the mailing date. Now either the U.S. Postal Service is getting slower in delivery or the credit card companies are slow in their processing of payments.

—Sharon Rayner

These guys are worse then Al Capone's street thugs. They might not beat you up physically, but they beat you up financially. They take advantage of stressed out people with large credit card debt.

—Herman C. Fields

These tales of abuse at the hands of credit card issuers were posted at the Federal Reserve Board's website. The Fed invited comments, of which these are just a sample, because it proposed improving Regulation Z (Truth in Lending) to make credit card terms and conditions clearer. As these personal stories indicate, consumers feel that truth in lending is far from clear. Regulation Z, with its absurd name, is mostly a joke—at the consumers' expense. Even Fed Chairman Ben Bernanke saw the need for change in the misleading world of credit cards, explaining, "The goal of the proposed revisions is to make sure that consumers get key information about credit card terms in a clear and conspicuous format and at a time when it would be most useful to them."

Consumers and credit card issuers are involved in a cat-and-mouse game centered on consumers' behavioral biases. Card companies, or at least some of them, try to outwit consumers by exploiting their psychological vulnerabilities and errors. The good news is consumers can and do learn to change their behavior. The bad news is firms preying on them do so as well and up the ante. But don't despair: It is possible to stay one or several steps ahead of even the most aggressive card issuer. Behavioral economics offers many insights and practical solutions for consumers grappling with credit card problems.

The Credit Card Business Model

Gail Hillebrand is a senior attorney at Consumers Union, the nonprofit consumer advocacy organization. She is lobbying to eliminate many standard industry practices that are damaging to consumers. Her point is these practices aren't incidental to the industry; they are at the heart of industry profits, because they are much more lucrative than plain vanilla lending. According to the fine print of most credit card agreements, the companies can essentially do anything they want, changing terms to suit themselves. And what suits the industry, argues Hillebrand, is to find ways to jack up fees and interest rates. An over-the-limit fee can be charged even when the card issuer approved the charge that put the account over the limit, or even when it is the finance charge that puts the account over the limit. Paying by phone carries a high fee, even though one reason consumers use it is to get the payment in on time. International foreign currency conversion carries unique extra fees as well. (These were hidden on statements until a class-action lawsuit forced card companies to disclose them.) Perhaps the most notorious penalty is what is known as "universal default": Even if you are paying your credit card bills on time but are late in paying a utility bill, the card company can jack up your interest rate.

"Their business model is to keep you in debt continually," Hillebrand told me. "I think this pricing model is based on exploiting consumer optimism." Here is the first behavioral vulnerability of consumers: You over-optimistically think your finances will be better in the future and it will be easier for you then to be able to repay bills. Or you think you will never forget to pay a bill, triggering penalties.

"The minimum owed" statements are typical of the PSYOPS (psychological operations) thrown at consumers. People anchor their payment to these minimums, not realizing how much they could save in interest in the long term by paying more. The amounts are kept artificially low and are designed to make it hard for consumers to climb out of debt. Hillebrand gives me an example: If you owe $10,000 on your credit card and pay the minimums required of you, it will take you 27 years to pay off your debt, at a 15% interest rate. You will have paid the credit card company an additional $11,979 in interest more than you originally borrowed. To make matters worse, if you already owe money, it's hard to move to a new card or leave your old card behind. You are stuck. (This is nothing compared to the tactics of mortgage lenders. The "option adjustable rate mortgage," marketed at some banks under the brand name "Pick-a-Pay," had monthly payments that did not even cover interest. The homeowner may have been under the impression they were paying off their mortgage but in fact the principal they owed kept growing over time.)

Snap Judgment and Interest Rates

The minimum owed is just one example of the card-issuing companies exploiting our intuitive perceptions and gut reaction. Our psychological vulnerabilities to credit cards are extensive and go well beyond poor impulse control, which is easily solved by cutting up your credit cards so you don't overspend. As the card companies are well aware, consumers are prone to one devastating bias in particular: We ignore the fact that interest compounds.

"Consumers make mistakes when borrowing, but what is more interesting is the mistakes are biased in a particular way: Consumers underestimate the true cost of borrowing," explains Jonathan Zinman, a behavioral economist at Dartmouth. Zinman studies how consumers make financial decisions, including how they use their credit cards. His research suggests consumers leave a serious amount of money on the table in both checking and credit cards by paying penalty fees that are avoidable, and by generally not using their lowest-cost payment or borrowing option. This does not make him an automatic critic of credit card issuers. In fact, quite the opposite: "Credit cards are a great product. They are convenient. Effectively they are very long maturity loans and are useful for many people," he says.

But people still have problems with credit cards and banks loans too, namely how we *perceive* the cost of borrowing. Says Zinman, "We have an intuitive tendency to underestimate how expensive it is to borrow and an intuitive tendency to underestimate how remunerative it is to save." This isn't about hidden fees; this occurs when such costs are fully disclosed. It is about interest, or more specifically the power of compounding. Zinman and his co-author Victor Stango have found that "consumers underestimate how quickly a given yield compounds, so they underestimate the expected future value of an investment." Similarly, they find that people systematically underestimate the loan interest rate they are paying if they have to try to guess it based on monthly payments due, principal, and maturity. Here is one of his examples: If you were borrowing $10,000 to buy a car and had quotes from two lenders, one for an APR of 8% and one for 48 monthly payments of $299, which is a better deal? This is not an easy calculation to do mentally. It turns out the second option is worse, much worse. It implies an APR of 20%, but most people would guess what they are paying is much lower—that is, if their eyes don't glaze over first.

Says Zinman, "People have sort of a cognitive bug. They systematically underestimate compound growth or decline." Stango and Zinman call this "fuzzy math." More formally they link it to extensive research in cognitive psychology on "exponential growth bias." This bias is that our intuitive thinking can't handle exponential functions such as compound interest. So when we try to intuit complex interest calculations, we tend to come up short. We straight line the amount we owe or the amount we are owed, underestimating the power of compounding. This means that when it comes to car loans, home equity loans, subprime products, and perhaps credit cards we pay down slowly over time, these products all appear deceptively cheap.

The Case of Shrouded Fees: Winning the Credit Card Game

Many consumers tired of being continually in debt or hit with strange fees, come to see the credit card business model for what it is. Some walk, unless they are already too much in debt to get away. For most of us, the nuisance of occasional late fees is more than offset by the convenience of credit cards. But it is possible to do even better, to beat the credit card companies at their own game, once you have figured out which behavioral tactics they are deploying.

Behavioral economists Xavier Gabaix of NYU and David Laibson of Harvard have looked deeply into the hidden fees and costs associated with various products. They call these hidden add-on prices "shrouded" prices. Credit cards are merely one of many products with shrouded prices; the better known example is computer printers. The price of a new printer may seem remarkably cheap. But really the low price is to hook you on the ink, which is not included in your printing price estimates. The company's real business is selling ink cartridges. Does HP come to mind? It should—in 2004, 30% of the company's revenues and much of its profits came from its "printing and imaging unit." However, customers who bought generic ink cartridges as a way around this problem could face a new type of shrouding: The generics may not be as good as the HP original. *Consumer Reports*, after testing generics, concluded: "Off brands often didn't cut photo costs much because they printed fewer photos than brand-name cartridges. Also, they generally didn't match the manufacturers' inks for print quality and fade resistance."

Airline travel is infested with shrouded pricing. Suppose you have a choice of two airlines. The fare on one is cheaper. But what the fare doesn't reveal is that it doesn't include any checked bags. Or lunch. Nor do you learn about the airline's deferred maintenance program for its "heritage" fleet of aging aircraft. These have all been shrouded, suppressed at the time of online purchase, where only the fare and schedule are immediately clear. (The schedule can involve shrouding, too. According to 2007 statistics from Flightstats.com, which records flight performance, only 74% of flights on the New York–to–Los Angeles route, for instance, arrived on time. Scheduled travel time for the route has increased, too, up on average 44 minutes from 30 years ago.)

Shrouding prices can involve add-ons that consumers have the possibility of avoiding, such as paying for lunch on a plane rather than bringing your own. Or it can involve hidden surcharges. Gabaix and Laibson's ideas mostly focus on the former.

Let's suppose you buy a super-cheap printer that "shrouds" the cost of printing, as opposed to a slightly more expensive one from a company that is more upfront about the costs, and maybe even offers cheaper inkjets over the long term. You were naive, taken advantage of, but you have learned the hard way. You also learned how to get your ink cartridges filled for very little money and at a place that actually has good ink. It comes time to buy a new printer. You are now more sophisticated. Do you go back to the super-cheap but misleading brand? The rational answer is yes.

As Gabaix and Laibson write, "Informed consumers...prefer to patronize—and in particular, exploit—firms that offer loss-leader prices on base-goods." Essentially, you go for the loss leader, but avoid all the shrouded costs the company assumes it will snare you with. You take the bait but don't get hooked on all the expensive hidden charges that follow because you are looking out for these.

Specifically, in terms of credit cards, Gabaix and Laibson suggest that an educated credit card holder target cards that offer convenience, float, and miles, while taking care to avoid paying interest charges and late fees. The issuer assumes you will screw up in some way, by using the credit card after the teaser rate has ended, for instance. And it's true that even the most sophisticated consumers can get taken in, because they can't be bothered to pay attention, or because they understand interest rates but not their own psychology and underestimate their likely inertia. But these caveats aside, for the educated and self-controlled consumer, it makes more sense to patronize the loss leader with lots of high fees waiting down the road, instead of the more straightforward product, if you are aware of these fees and can find a way around them. So look for the cards that have fantastic teaser rates or incredible airline miles bonuses—these can be better deals for the sophisticated consumer.

The economics behind this model is that the naive consumers are cross-subsidizing the sophisticated ones. Credit card users who get snared by teaser rates or immense late fees are paying for the loss-leading teaser rates in the first place. The sophisticated consumer and the underhanded card company both profit at the naive consumers' expense.

It takes a lot of time to keep track of various credit card offers and schemes, but for many people it's worth it. For instance, I have a friend in New York who spends each summer at a private island off of Sweden. He spends each winter patiently obtaining different cards for their introductory air-miles bonus and then immediately discards them. This means he goes through many cards because he will only fly first class. When I questioned him about why he insisted on first class given all the extra miles and cards he had to accumulate, he told me it really comes down to economics. Taking a page from Graham Greene, he claims the better wine served in first class makes the upgrade pay for itself.

24

Snap Judgment and Social Security: When Should You Claim It?

Choosing the age to start Social Security is probably the most important financial decision you will make in your life. All too often, though, it is an impulsive snap judgment with dire consequences—not for the breadwinner making the decision, but for the spouse.

Here are some financial facts that should go into the decision. For the average American, Social Security covers slightly more than 40% of monthly expenses. Currently, you can claim Social Security benefits starting at age 62 up until 70. The longer you wait, the higher the amount you get. Each year you wait, the amount you receive goes up by approximately another 7%. A four-year delay gets you about one-third more per check. So the decision is, Do you want a larger annuity starting later or a smaller annuity starting now?

Most economics models suggest delaying Social Security as the single best way to guarantee against low living standards in old age. Social Security, despite its flaws and problems, has some amazing features. It is actuarially fair. It is inflation adjusted, which is a feature very difficult to get in your other investments. Inflation could melt away your bonds and your other annuities, but not Social Security. And, last but not least, Social Security has survivor benefits. The lower-earning wife (or husband) is entitled to the higher-earning deceased spouse's monthly check in place of their own. The exact rules about this are complex, but this is the general idea.

Here is how most people make the decision: They get it as soon as they can. For men, half claim by 62 or 63. Many people have no other choice; they need the money now, or they might be in poor health and are not certain to live much longer. Others may worry that Social Security won't last—the system after all is shaky financially.

For men, on average, the timing of their decision isn't a mistake financially. If some men claim early and live a long time on low payments, this is balanced out by men who claim late and don't last very long but receive higher payments. The way Social Security is structured, this is all taken into account; the change in payments reflects the change in risks. One of these is that men tend to die sooner than their wives.

The real problem has to do with the wives. Claiming early may be the right decision for men, but because of survivor benefits, their spouses will be negatively impacted. The widows will have to live out the rest of their lives on a reduced Social Security check because their husbands claimed early, and the financial differences can be large. A widow whose husband claimed at 66 (today's "full retirement age") will likely get a check at least one-third greater than a widow whose husband claimed at 62. Analysis from the Boston College Center for Retirement Research shows "as many elderly widows have very low incomes, early claiming by married men is a major social problem."

"Frankly, the behavior of married men is just plain weird," says Steven Sass, of the Center for Retirement Research. "I think many people just don't think about the implications," Sass tells me. "What happens is you are working in your 50s or early 60s and a new boss shows up and you are pissed. Or you come back from vacation, and you realize you don't really like your job. If you were 40 or 50, you could go on. But you decide to retire and to take Social Security. Claiming Social Security is too much of an impulsive decision."

It is not clear if married men aren't aware of the impact of their decision on survivor benefits, or simply don't care. What is clear is that men are relying on snap judgments or at best superficial calculations rather than thinking through the consequences of their decision of when to start Social Security. Money now intuitively seems better than money later. Or waiting is framed as a risky gamble—you might die today and never get to collect Social Security—rather than a prudent way of insuring financial security for you and your spouse in later years. A lot of this is social convention as well. When most people retire, they start Social Security immediately. It seems automatic, but it doesn't have to be. Maybe public policy, instead of pushing abstinence and delaying sex until marriage, should instead promote delaying claiming Social Security. It would help out married women a lot.

At the very least, when thinking about when to claim Social Security, you should consider the impact of the start date on your survivor's benefits as well as your own. To do this you will need to use a retirement calculator, of which there are thousands to choose from. The joke in the retirement policy community is there are more retirement calculators than porn sites. (Yes, there is a retirement policy community. And, yes, they tell jokes, although of course not very often.) Unfortunately, almost none of the calculators automatically includes survivor benefits. Social Security's own calculator is a good one to start with. It doesn't factor in survivor benefits on its own, so you will have to run the numbers first on yourself, and then rerun on them your spouse to make a full determination of when it is most advantageous to start Social Security.

25

How Patients Think Irrationally

Richard S. felt short of breath, couldn't stop sweating, and had a strange headache. The 40-something truck driver was aware of the warning signs of a heart attack—he had suffered from several, so he went to the nearest emergency room, at Foote Hospital in Jackson, Michigan. Richard was all too experienced with the health system. In addition to his heart attacks, he had uncontrolled hypertension and was recovering from a stroke.

The emergency medicine attending at the time was Dr. Kirsten Engel, who was also working on a research fellowship. Here are her notes about "Richard" from that night (I have changed the patient's identifying details):

> "The patient before me was a 40-year-old man with a history of poorly controlled hypertension, heart disease, and stroke. On initial assessment, it was clear that this patient was experiencing a hypertensive emergency and it was my impression that associated intracranial hemorrhage, MI, and aortic dissection needed to be ruled out. After I had completed the history and examination, I proceeded to outline my thoughts and differential diagnosis in an effort to explain to the patient the need for blood pressure medications, further testing with x-rays, Cat Scans (CT), and blood work, and ultimately admission to the hospital....
>
> I explained [to] this patient the need for a chest CT in order to rule out a possible tear in the large blood vessel that leaves the heart."

Dr. Engel left Richard with a nurse at his bedside in order to attend to another emergency. When she checked back in with the patient to see if he was willing to go ahead with the CT, she found a commotion. Richard had misunderstood her discussion of the chest CT to mean, in his words, "His heart was ripping open." Turning from the patient, Dr. Engel asked the nurse about his blood pressure. The nurse snapped, "Well, I am not going to be able to get his blood pressure under control if you keep telling him that he is dying."

It was only at that point that Dr. Engel understood how Richard had heard her clinical assessment—as a painful death sentence. As she wrote that night: "Unfortunately, my words had only served to generate confusion and intensify his anxiety and concern." Eventually she was able to clear up the confusion and allay his anxiety. Richard had a serious heart problem, but his heart wasn't ripping open. He was admitted to the hospital and survived.

Richard S.'s story, of patient misperception under high stress, is typical. Dr. Engel, like most clinicians, has noticed it again and again, as well as how it affects patients' decisions. Engel mentions a situation with another patient that is all too typical. She asked the wife of an elderly patient who was in the midst of a stroke if she would consent to giving him thrombolytics, clot-busting meds that could alleviate a stroke but carried substantial risks. The wife, a composed-looking, well-spoken Midwestern housewife went blank. She became almost catatonic. Faced with the potential death of her husband, the wife "literally began to shake, was unable to process information to make a decision," Engel remembers. (Her husband improved while in the ER, so the thrombolytics in the end weren't necessary.)

Concerned, but also intrigued by these common patient reactions, Engel began a systematic study of patients' understanding of their emergency department care. The study found that only "22 percent of patients' reports were in complete harmony with their care team," in terms of comprehending their diagnosis, emergency department (ED) care, post-ED care, and return instructions. It is easy to understand why emergency department patients don't take in the information given to them. They are in emotional and possibly physical shock, while being overwhelmed with information delivered in incomprehensible medical jargon. It's not clear why it has taken medicine so long to recognize this. But most patients are themselves not aware of the problem. Engel's study found most patients were unaware of their lack of understanding of discharge instructions and "report inappropriate confidence in their comprehension and recall."

In the recent past, the fact that patients had trouble comprehending information or didn't think clearly in high-stress situations was less urgent. No one really asked them for their input, certainly not to the same degree as today. Take cancer: Prior to the 1960s doctors might not even tell a patient they had cancer or perhaps obliquely mention that there was a "fuzzy picture on the lungs." Then the consumer movement and its equivalent in healthcare, the patient's rights movement, insisted that patients deserved more information, although doctors still made most of the decisions. Today patients are closely involved in treatment decisions themselves. Mastectomy versus lumpectomy? Radiation or surgery for prostate cancer? In the past the doctor dictated. Now, in theory at least, the doctor calls upon the patients for input of what is important to them and how they would like to balance the benefits and side effects of each treatment.

This new movement is known as "shared decision making." The focus is on "preference sensitive decisions"—when there is a choice among several interventions in which the right choice depends on a patient's preferences. This doesn't have to involve things with equal odds of survival. Sometimes one intervention leads to longer survival, but at a lower quality of life. It is up to an individual patient to decide how to make this tradeoff. For instance, breast cancer can be treated with a complete mastectomy, or a lumpectomy and radiation. The importance the patient places on retaining their breast is a factor in deciding what to do.

"It's great that patient preferences now actually matter and that we are informing people," says Dr. Peter Ubel, a Professor of Medicine and Psychology at the University of Michigan. "But we still need to be aware of how people are influenced. We need to think carefully of what can go wrong." Ubel is a leader, but also a critic, of the emerging field of shared decision making. He has authored numerous studies on how patient decisions are highly influenced by "framing." For instance, if doctors give patients information about the risks of a drug followed by benefits, it leads to very different choices than if the information is presented in the opposite order. "Nothing is neutral," he says.

The fundamental computation biases that show up in financial decisions are present in patients' medical decisions, too. Patients, or rather people, are notoriously bad at understanding risks and probabilities, particularly for dreaded diseases that are widely discussed in the media. The average woman believes her risk of getting breast cancer during her lifetime is 40%. In fact, it is closer to 13%. Similarly, men overestimate the risk of getting prostate cancer. And people are influenced by anecdotes and celebrities. After Nancy Reagan had a mastectomy, the American mastectomy rates went up, particularly for women in the South and West. Following Katie Couric's televised colonoscopy, the number of colonoscopies shot up.

Even where doctors strive for neutrality in presenting information, the patient still may not be taking in any of it. Says Ubel, "I think when a doctor says, 'You have cancer. Here is your five-year odds of survival without treatment. How would you like to treat it? Surgery or radiation?' the patient just hears 'cancer blah blah blah cancer.'" The ER study by Dr. Engel, of which Ubel was a coauthor, demonstrated that not only were emergency room patients uninformed, they didn't know they didn't have a clue.

Ideally, Ubel feels doctors should present patients with treatment choices and statistical information on a follow-up visit when the patient is calmer, leaving any important decisions until that time. Says Ubel, "A new cancer diagnosis is no time for a patient to make a decision. The focus of the first visit should be helping patients deal with potentially devastating news." In reality, however, patients may not have the luxury of multiple visits with a doctor to calmly evaluate different treatment choices.

So here is what you can do: Bring someone to the doctor with you. Or even bring a tape recorder. "The reality is, the more afraid you are, the more likely you are not going to comprehend new information and make a bad decision," says Ubel. Having a friend or relative with you may be the only way around this likelihood.

But make sure it is a *calm* friend or relative. Mark Schlesinger, a health economist at Yale who studies patient decision making, points out families are more emotional than the person with the disease. Dying patients who have wrestled with the idea and then have finally chosen a "do not resuscitate directive" are routinely overruled by hysterical relatives.

Another strategy to improve medical self-decision making, the only truly effective one, according to Schlesinger, is to find a support group. "Information is most richly shared by survivors of the condition involved," he says. Here someone facing a decision can talk to someone who has already made it. That person may have made the wrong decision. But at the very least he or she has already been through the process—including perhaps the initial panic and lack of comprehension—and can take you past this, to see life beyond the diagnosis.

26

Health Insurance Decisions

Choosing health insurance is a situation where the stakes are high, the decision is complex, and there is a lot of anxiety about making the right choice. Also, picking a plan isn't something we encounter frequently—once a year at most—so we aren't familiar with the nuances of what each plan really covers. The elements involved—health and money—combined with uncertainty about what we are choosing makes for an unpleasant and possibly upsetting situation. When faced with this sort of dilemma, most people would rather avoid the situation altogether and not make any decision at all. Or we rely on our gut instinct to guide us, which can easily come up short.

This all-too-natural tendency has consequences when it comes to picking health insurance, as it does elsewhere in our financial lives. It means we are less effective consumers. Our own choices don't serve our best interests. But it also shifts the balance of power to the insurance industry. The industry is aware of our limitations and reacts accordingly, to serve its own financial interests.

Medicare Part D, which deals with prescription drug coverage, is an example of how difficult health insurance choices can be. Nationally there are over 1,800 plans. At the state level, the choices facing individuals range from selecting among 45 plans (residents of Alaska) to a high of 61 (residents of Pennsylvania). With the average enrollee needing five prescription drugs, there are even more cost and coverage factors to juggle than these numbers suggest.

The U.S. government is aware the choices facing enrolling consumers in Part D can be bewildering, even overwhelming. So it
launched a cheerfully packaged informational campaign to explain
Part D using the simplest possible language, titled "America, pull up
a chair. We've got something good to talk about."

I pulled up a chair and started reading the accompanying website to
see how it could possibly simplify the Part D decision. It told me there
are just "four steps you can think about while making a decision" about
Part D. What could these be? Ominous overtones of the four horsemen
of the apocalypse came to mind. Or perhaps the brochure would suggest a modified version of a "twelve step" recovery program only
applied to Medicare. (A founding principle of 12-step programs,
"admitting that one cannot control one's addiction or compulsion,"
could be a perversely appropriate way to describe the relationship
between some of the elderly and their prescription medications.)
Instead, the first step, "Getting started," used language that started off
easy but soon become impenetrable:

> "Most people with Medicare pay for drugs and get their
> Medicare in one of five ways: Original Medicare only, or
> Original Medicare and a Medigap ('Supplement') Policy
> without drug coverage. The new Medicare drug coverage will
> cover half of the costs for you if you have this kind of coverage
> now. Enhanced options are available that provide more cov-
> erage; Original Medicare and a Medigap ('Supplement') Pol-
> icy with drug coverage. The new Medicare drug coverage will
> generally provide much more comprehensive coverage at a
> lower cost; Medicare Advantage Plan (like an HMO or PPO)
> or other Medicare Health Plan, which already include drug
> coverage and other extra benefits...."

You get the picture. The second step, "Determining what matters
most and reviewing plan options" was equally difficult:

> "There are a range of plan options available, so you can focus
> on the kind of coverage you prefer.... You can add drug cover-
> age to the traditional Medicare plan through a "stand alone"
> prescription drug plan. Or you can get drug coverage and the

rest of your Medicare coverage through a Medicare Advantage plan, like an HMO or PPO, that typically provides more
benefits at a significantly lower cost through a network of
doctors and hospitals."

These two steps were merely introductions to the real problem—
of choosing and enrolling in a plan (steps 3 and 4)—at which point
the website directed me to further websites for help. Although the
"America, pull up a chair" campaign attempts to make all this choice
in Part D sound easy, it isn't. This isn't just my impression: The U.S.
Government Accountability office drew similar conclusions about
Part D. Congressional testimony by economists Richard Frank and
Joseph Newhouse of Harvard, based on GAO findings, stated: "This
complexity has potentially discouraged some enrollment, created
confusion, and likely led to choices of coverage that are not cost effective."

I spoke to Richard Frank, who specializes in the economics of
mental health treatment in addition to having an interest in health
insurance choice. He had helped his own mother navigate Part D. It
took her three hours—with his help. Faced with 45 choices, her
impulse was to go with a plan that she had heard of, only it didn't
cover her prescription. Eventually, she found a plan that provided
better coverage for less cost, but so did a lot of other people. Adverse
selection hit the plan hard and it disappeared after a year.

Frank explained to me, "One of the things that occurs in health
insurance decisions is inertia. People don't like to choose, and once
they do they don't switch. You see this in Medicare Part D."

Our inertia creates huge opportunities for insurance companies.
They can raise prices because they know we don't like to switch plans
and have to face the unpleasant and complex health insurance decision all over again. All they have to do is lure us in, in the first place.
This situation is comparable to credit card companies that use teaser
rates to attract us, then start jacking up prices. Only health insurance
is infinitely more complex than credit cards. Says Frank, "As insurers

learn about these frictions in the market, they behave accordingly. They raise prices because they know they won't lose a share of the action."

This ability of insurers to exploit our psychological confusion and inertia caused by too many choices has been most thoroughly studied in Switzerland, which is sometimes held up as a free market utopia for health insurance. Switzerland has a highly competitive health insurance market. Consumers really do have freedom to choose their insurer; it isn't locked in through their employer. And here is the result of all the choice. Frank and a colleague found that "as the number of choices offered to individuals grow, their willingness to switch plans declined." This created large price differences among relatively similar plans as some plans hiked up their prices.

This worries public policy experts like Frank: "The question is, how naked do you leave the consumer in the marketplace. Do you leave them alone? Or with very little guidance with information, which is Medicare? Or do you do what employers do and do pre-screening and pre-bargaining?"

Here is what consumers can do—use an insurance broker. You could, of course, do it yourself, but unless you want to spend a lot of time sorting out health insurance, you can outsource the problem to someone whose job specialty is to deal with this unpleasant and time-consuming decision. They won't exhibit the same fear about evaluating and switching plans. Some states have tried to eliminate brokers; alternatively some financial planners now offer this valuable service. The best evidence in their favor comes from Switzerland. In Switzerland, people who used brokers to help them with their health insurance ending up paying much less.

27

Car Accidents

We know that small errors in intuitive judgments can lead to irreparable consequences. This is true in our investment choices, deciding when to retire, or to double down in Blackjack. But motor vehicle crashes are a clearer and more present danger. When you make an error in reasoning or a faulty decision when you are driving, it can change your life forever.

Dr. Donald Redelmeier is an internist at Sunnybrook Health Sciences Centre in Toronto who treats trauma victims and their injuries, such as shattered skulls, fractures, organ rupture, and internal bleeding. Redelmeier has an additional line of work: He has a background in cognitive psychology, studying errors in medical reasoning. One of his early studies found a widely and strongly held belief among arthritis patients that their pain is somehow influenced by the weather. Careful statistical tracking has found no such correlation. Instead, patients are seeing patterns where none exist, in the same way that investors read patterns or even stories into stock market behavior. Redelmeier explains to his patients that if they were to move to the dry climate of Arizona in the hope of their arthritis disappearing, they will be sorely disappointed.

Redelmeier's current research is focused on driving. His clinical experience in trauma, with the leading cause of trauma being car accidents, led him to apply his interest in errors in reasoning to this area. As he explained to me, "Our faulty intuition and easy distractibility are the cause of many car accidents."

This can be something as simple as deciding to change lanes on the expressway, which is the common cause of many accidents. We do so because of an intuitive mistake. The main reason drivers change lanes is because the other lane is moving faster. When we are stuck in a traffic jam, it always *looks* like our lane is moving slower and the other lane is faster. This isn't just our perception—it is every driver's perception. But in fact it is a misperception, an optical illusion.

Redelmeier walks me through his research: "Our studies show an optical illusion develops that makes the next lane in a traffic jam to seem to be faster than the driver's current lane. The illusion is strongest under high degrees of congestion. A misunderstanding of the law of statistics leads people to make unnecessary changes where risks are real but the benefits few."

The illusion derives from the physics of traffic flows and our intuitive perception of movement. Cars traveling slowly tend to be closely packed together. When traffic moves smoothly and quickly, more space opens up between each vehicle. If you are in a lane that momentarily slows down, traffic immediately becomes congested, whereas in the lane that is still moving, there are lots of open spaces between vehicles.

This disparity in spacing plays on our perceptions. From the point of view of the driver in the fast lane, five or six cars in the slow lane all go by in a single clump, because the slow cars are all packed together. Now consider what happens when the fast lane slows for a few seconds and traffic picks up in the other lane. The cars in the other lane are now widely separated from each other and seem quite distinct. First one car zooms by, then a pause, then another. The perception of the driver in what was the fast lane is that he is being overtaken by six cars. He can make out each one.

The normal ebbs and flow in traffic appear to be unbalanced. You only pass one clump when things are moving well in your lane, but are overtaken by six cars from the other lane whey they aren't. This can become excruciating. You always feel like you are in the slower lane.

"What this means is every trip contains relatively few moments of pleasure and a lot more moments of aggravation. The asymmetry holds for every drive: The grass is always greener in the next lane," says the good doctor. This leads drivers to change lanes as opposed to just sitting tight. Changing lanes disrupts traffic flows in two lanes: The one you are leaving and the one you are entering. Drivers face blind spots as well. Each lane switch is linked to a threefold increase of a crash, all the result of misperceptions.

Redelmeier's interest in driving fatalities has led him to study other situations where crashes tend to occur, such as Super Bowl Sunday. The real trauma takes place off the field—in the traffic on the way home. Driving on Super Bowl Sunday is more dangerous than New Year's Eve. There is a surge in fatalities shortly after the game is over. Although it occurs nationwide, it is not evenly distributed. It is more pronounced in states with losing teams and somewhat attenuated in states that have fielded the winning team.

Redelmeier's diagnosis: "Monday Morning quarterbacking occurs Sunday night. Drivers get distracted." Alcohol is in part to blame, with fans of losing teams consoling themselves with drink. But the deeper reason for the difference in deaths between fans of losing and winning teams is the way we think about losses. As in financial decisions, losses loom larger than gains, and we tend to dwell more on our failures than successes. We become distracted and less focused on driving. The aggravation of losing, the distractions it causes, leads to a truly poignant outcome—a fatal crash.

There are some public policy solutions for our cognitive problems associated with driving. (Elections, though, are not one of them. Election night is even more dangerous for driving than Super Bowl Sunday, according to Redelmeier. Although he has noticed no discernable differences in fatalities between Democrats and Republicans, Southern males are at increased risk on election night.) Better traffic enforcement is one solution. Drivers who receive a speeding ticket experience a 30% decrease in car crashes the following months. The slap on the wrist has a deterrent effect, making people better drivers. But the deterrent effect doesn't last very long. Drivers return to their old behavior within two to three months. In North America, the average driver receives a ticket only every five years. "That argues for much more automated enforcement technologies such as cameras and photo radar. The problem, though, is enforcement is such a public relations loser," points out Redelmeier. People don't like it.

For the individual worried about car crashes, there are some answers. Don't talk on the phone. (Eating seems to present less of a danger because you can wolf down bites quickly, albeit inelegantly, and you can time your bites so they don't interfere with, say, changing lanes.) Regardless of the state you are living in, or the emotional state you are in, don't drive on Super Bowl Sunday. The key is to avoid any sort of cognitive or emotional overload.

I asked Redelmeier, with his multiple research studies and first-hand knowledge of both trauma and driver psychology, what he suggested to overcome the intuitive errors we are prone to make on the road. His response was not the counterintuitive, complex finding I expected. Instead, it just made a lot of sense. Said Dr. Redelmeier: "One of the secrets of driving is not to be in a rush. If you want to arrive 15 minutes earlier, leave 15 minutes sooner."

Part IV
CEO Behavior

CEOs are a breed apart. The average salary of a CEO is now about 344 times that of the average U.S. worker. Thirty years ago it was only 30 times greater than the typical employee's salary. During his divorce proceedings, it was revealed that Jack Welch, the retired CEO of GE, in addition to his multimillion-dollar pension, was entitled to the use of the corporate jet and the provision of daily fresh flowers for his Manhattan apartment at GE's expense. (Welch has since agreed to pay for the flowers out of his own pocket). A CEO of a very small company I once worked for, with no corporate jet, insisted that her luggage be FedEx'ed whenever she traveled so she didn't have to carry anything.

A hard-edged analysis of the behavior of CEOs is a newer branch of behavioral economics. The focus is on corporate strategy and profitability, identifying ways CEOs make or break companies. It turns out much of CEO behavior is fully predictable. It also goes astray in certain recognizable patterns. The idols of the business world often have feet of clay. Nowhere is this so true as on Wall Street, where CEOs, and their increasingly risky gambles during the years leading up to the financial crisis, broke their own banks. The rest of the country was left to clean up the trillion-dollar mess they made. But what is noteworthy is that even amid the overall failure of the investment banking industry, a handful of CEOs were skillful at managing their institutions during the upheaval. What accounts for their relative success?

The following chapters look at what makes CEOs tick and how they and their boards rely on intuition instead of rational analysis. It is based on new insights gleaned from recent behavioral economics research.

28

Strategic "Styles"

The main conclusion arising out of the new field of economics that studies CEO behavior is quite simple. CEOs, even if they bill themselves as "change agents," are themselves almost always unable to change. CEOs are inflexible in their strategic vision, whatever it may be. They manage with certain styles, largely regardless of market conditions and needs. They are the products of their experience, and some become victims of their experiences, unable to adopt new points of view. Perhaps this is why Wall Street CEOs had so much trouble accepting the party was over, and continued to pay themselves bonuses and luxuriously refurbish their offices as if the crisis had never happened.

The rigorous, statistical identification of predictable patterns of CEO behavior and how they affect performance is largely the work of Antoinette Schoar, an economist at MIT. Schoar has shown that how aggressive a company is in trying to grow and how it finances its growth are ultimately *personal* decisions: They are all about who happens to be CEO. Also, there are certain clusters of CEO behavior. Aggressive CEOs who are trying to grow the company use more leverage (using debt or borrowed capital to increase returns), hold less cash, and are more likely to try external acquisitions rather than internal research and development as a means for growth. Conservative CEOs tend to hold more cash, use less leverage on the balance sheet, and grow through internal investments rather than acquisitions. These different styles make a difference in terms of corporate performance. Aggressive

CEOs have a higher rate of return on assets than conservative CEOs, unless the aggressive ones have undertaken a lot of acquisitions. This last point is the fatal flaw in many CEOs' strategies.

Why Andy Grove Fired Himself

Intel's Andy Grove is an exception to the general rule that CEOs are inflexible in their strategic styles. Today, Intel is a dominant force in the computer world; its microprocessors run 80% of the world's personal computers. This success story, which seems so obvious now, was far from assured. In the mid-1980s, the company was facing deadly competition from Japanese chip manufacturers and it looked like Intel might not survive. At a crossroads, Intel needed to reinvent itself and move in a new strategic direction. Andy Grove, Intel's founder, made the tough decision to fire the CEO—himself. He then hired a new CEO—himself.

Grove later wrote, "Intel faced what I call a strategic inflection point. What is a strategic inflection point? It is a word or a phrase to describe major discontinuity in your business, a discontinuity that comes, creeps up on you fairly gradually and unless you change gears, shift gears, you will be in trouble." His self-firing and hiring marked the shift in gears (no word on a golden parachute, or the new salary), and it worked. The company left memory chips behind and instead intensively developed and then dominated the lucrative microprocessor market. Most PCs now say "Intel inside."

I spoke to Schoar, asking what her analysis meant for those of us on the outside, or inside, trying to figure out what a particular CEO is up to. (Schoar, like many researchers I interviewed for this book, wanted to be clear that she shouldn't be pigeon-holed as a behavioral economist. However, she does use behavioral tools for some of her work including her analysis of CEOs.)

"I think a lot of CEO behavior is like the phrase, 'For the man with a hammer, every problem looks like a nail.' Many CEOs, when they go to a new firm do exactly what they did at the last one. They use the same degree of financial leverage, they go with either the aggressive or conservative approach they used last time," Schoar says. That is why their strategic style—and to some degree performance— is largely predictable. Turnaround artists pursue turnarounds, cost cutters cut costs. The more interesting finding is Schoar's conclusion about which styles tend to fail and which ones are more likely to succeed: "We find that managers who are very aggressive in terms of takeovers and mergers, who diversify their firm, tend to have much lower performance across time and in most situations."

And yet they keep getting hired. It is, of course, a case of falling upward, but why do corporate boards make this sort of mistake? And why can't CEOs, who by definition have what it takes to climb the greasy pole of corporate life, make the necessary adjustments to their new situation? Why aren't they rational enough to adjust? "It's kind of weird," says Schoar. "It's as if people and people's decisions are hardwired. We think we have the ability to change, but people seem set on a certain path."

Here the story gets very sociological. CEOs, like all of us, are the product of specific circumstances. Early influences in their career have lasting effects. Schoar says, "What I find is that if you look at someone who later becomes a CEO, whether they started their career in a depression or boom matters. CEOs who started working in a recession, once they become CEOs, tend to be much more conservative, using less leverage and making less acquisitions." In contrast, boom-era CEOs have a much more aggressive style.

The starting point also determined the course of their career paths. Everyone Schoar studied has ended up a CEO, but those who started in a recession era took a lot longer to get there. They tended to stay in one firm for many years and gradually rose through internal promotions. The boom-era beginners had much faster and easier careers and bounced around more. And people who started at specific firms had the fastest career later: Schoar's data pinpoints GE and Merrill Lynch as particularly good launching pads.

Much of this is surprising. We know generations are different, but we didn't know the corporate face of this. Moreover, the research pins down some of the irrationalities in corporate life. Says Schoar, "Either firms don't pay attention or don't differentiate enough between the environmental effects and ability. If you start in a recession and the firm isn't growing much, nobody looks stellar. You might be doing a fantastic job managing shrinking sales, whereas in a boom you might be doing a bad job but still doubling sales. But firms tend to promote people more in boom times, and these managers are also hired more by outside firms, which is behavioral (meaning irrational)."

Corporate boards don't seem fully aware of these behavioral patterns either. They hire a new CEO who behaves exactly the way he did on his last job, and the board is shocked to find they have a cost cutter or acquisition guy on their hands. Take, for example, the case of Al "Chainsaw" Dunlap, the former CEO of Sunbeam. Dunlap was a celebrated CEO, a self-identified cost cutter who had done extremely well in his prior CEO jobs. During his reign of cost cutting at Scott Paper, the stock price rose by over 200% in just 18 months. At Sunbeam he pursued the same strategy—draconian cuts in the workforce—with Dunlap trying to eliminate half of all employees. He encouraged managers not to get "weak kneed" when lining up employees for the corporate firing squad. But this time around Dunlap's cost-cutting strategy misfired. Sunbeam's stock crashed as a result. At Sunbeam, Dunlap's style and the company's culture really clashed. Cost cutting led to a huge problem for the firm, its stock price, and ultimately Dunlap, too: Eventually he was the one who was cut.

There is something gloomy about Schoar's finding. It shows how much of our careers are dependent on the luck of timing, which is something we might already now. But if CEOs' strategic styles are any guide, it also suggests how hard it is to adapt. We are like the leopard that can't change its spots. This is the opposite of everything we hear from Oprah. The entire self-help industry has a completely different message—that anyone can change, that change is good.

Apparently CEOs aren't listening to that message. But maybe because they are already at the CEO level they don't think they need to change; the rest of the world has to change to suit them.

29

CEO Hubris

Another pitfall of CEO behavior is overconfidence—which is really just a measured way of describing their extreme hubris. CEOs, by definition, have had a lot of success in their lives, certainly by the time they are CEOs. This can cross over into a feeling of invincibility, with their corporations—and investors—paying the price.

This largely psychological explanation has been put forward as to why the "urge to merge" is so widespread among CEOs, even though it is widely documented that mergers and acquisitions are generally bad news for the acquiring company, immensely bad. Subsequent to a merger, companies typically display negative returns, abnormally negative returns. The destruction to shareholder value is outrageous: Declines in stock prices following mergers resulted in investors in the acquiring firm losing $220 billion in the 1980s and 1990s, a corporate catastrophe only dwarfed by the Wall Street crisis in 2008 and 2009. The list of failed or underperforming mergers is without end. Think of AOL/Time Warner, Sprint/Nextel, Alcatel/Lucent, Daimler Benz/Chrysler, just for starters. This last one did so badly that it was subsequently dissolved. During the darkest days of the crisis, in the Fall 2008, the value of canceled M&A deals approached the size of deals that were actually completed during this period.

Mergers are so predictably damaging to acquiring firms' stock prices that you can make money betting against them. Hedge funds and some mutual funds do this all the time. You can track the impact on the stock price of the acquiring firm following the announcement of a merger: It is on average a negative number. The widespread and easily anticipated declines makes mergers and acquisitions, for the acquiring company, a clear example of what behavioral economists term "the winner's curse," the phenomenon where seeming winners in a merger or auction do badly afterward.

Serial Mergerers

Growing through mergers and acquisitions can pose problems for both corporations as well as their CEOs. Take, for instance, the example of Eckhard Pfeiffer, a name now forgotten. Although he may not be in the news much anymore, once he was the CEO of the late, and apparently not so great, computer company Compaq. Under his regime his objective was to make Compaq the #1 PC company, and he did this through mergers. He acquired Digital Equipment Corp for $8 billion in order to grow his company. Following the acquisition, the joint company floundered. Pfeiffer blamed his problem on rival IBM's "targeted action" of price cutting to undermine Compaq. *Fortune* magazine blamed Pfeiffer and his strategic vision, noting that "other PC makers are fine." Pfeiffer was fired, but it was too late. The company was forced to merge with Hewlett-Packard, led by another aggressive acquisition-minded CEO, Carly Fiorina. Fiorina herself was soon fired when her strategies failed to deliver.

Which brings us back to hubris. Mergers rarely work out for the best, yet CEOs persist in attempting them. Which, from a cold, dispassionate perspective, is interesting, even puzzling. "One may call a CEO who...does too many and bad mergers simply 'stupid' or low-skilled," writes the Berkeley behavioral economist Ulrike Malmendier.

Malmendier herself rejects the notion that mergers result from simple stupidity. She has indentified instead, through an ingenious feat of behavioral economics research, the psychological factor that is really behind many mergers: CEO overconfidence. She has found that CEOs who undertake mergers tend to be overconfident in many identifiable ways. They overestimate future returns from their newly merged company in the face of all evidence to the contrary. They also feel the market is undervaluing their company, and so they don't often issue stock or even borrow from the bank, preferring to rely on internal cash flows instead. But it is CEOs' personal investing decisions that are most revealing and even predictive about their tendency to undertake mergers. Overconfident CEOs tend to hold on to their executive stock options rather than diversifying their stock portfolio, as any financial planner would suggest. In another words, they are too bullish about their company. And they seem to have few inhibitions from acting on this sunny belief—namely, they undertake too many mergers. Alternatively, in the case of the demise of the Wall Street investment banks, the CEOs refused to believe their whole company could go under.

Malmendier explained it to me this way: "Being corporate insiders you may think these CEOs who hold on to their options and hold excessive company stock may know something. It all sounds good for shareholders, but it isn't." All that it really reveals is a measure of CEO overconfidence. The returns from most mergers are bad, but the returns from mergers undertaken by these "overconfident" CEOs are strikingly bad. Adds Malmendier, "Overconfident CEOs are unambiguously more likely to make lower-quality acquisitions when their firm has abundant internal resources and, in particular, destroy value for their shareholders through acquisitions." About 15% of CEOs fall into the overconfident category. Worried investors, therefore, need to see if there is an "overconfident" CEO at the helm. The way to do this is to track their CEO's personal investment decisions. Again, most CEOs already hold vast amounts of their own company stock; this is how they are often compensated, and investors often track this, even though it reveals little. Instead, Malmendier's measure is more precise: It is the *unexercised* vested options the CEO is holding that are crucial. If the CEO holds them to maturity (typically 10 years) without exercising them, then excessive optimism is at work. Conventional financial wisdom holds that investing in your company is a vote of confidence; the newer wisdom from behavioral economics

is that overinvesting in your company by delaying exercising your
options because you think the stock can only go up is just a sign of
overconfidence.

Superstar CEOs

Overconfident, filled with hubris, set in their ways—this
describes the strategic behavior of most CEOs. But there is a special
category of CEO, a subspecies if you will, superstar CEOs. These are
the CEOs on talk shows and the covers of the business press holding
forth on the issue of the day. The ones who appear at the World Economic Forum at Davos. The ones seemingly more worried about
global carbon emissions rather than their company's immediate
future. Although it is clear they are concerned global citizens, what is
less clear is if they are good for business: How does having a superstar
as CEO affect company value?

Superstars exist in other arenas than business, of course; they
aren't unique to the corporate context, so we can look elsewhere at
the long-term performance of stars. There is the nagging suspicion
that being pronounced a "superstar" only sets up the star in question
for subsequent disappointment and outright failures. "The *Sports
Illustrated* jinx" refers to the setbacks and worse that inevitably follow
being on the cover of *Sports illustrated.* In documentary films, the
winner of the Oscar always seems to spend the next year unem-
ployed. Academics refer to the "Nobel prize disease." After winning a
Nobel, the academic (who at this point often divorces his first wife)
spends the rest of his life crisscrossing the globe, "preaching to the
world on ethics and futurology, politics and philosophy," to quote
Paul Samuelson, never producing any important work again.

Economists, who like to view themselves as hard-headed types,
might argue these "jinxes" are just a statistical illusion. What is driving
the bad luck is really just a case of reversion to the mean, a return to
the average. Athletes get on the cover of *Sports Illustrated* following

a fantastic year, but in following years they just revert to their average and more typical performance. In the same way, you can't expect a Nobel Prize winner to have a great discovery every year. And similarly, superstar CEOs, those on the cover of business magazines, could be expected to have a few bad or at least average years following stellar performance.

But the story isn't so simple. The story is actually worse. Superstar CEOs underperform by a substantially larger margin than can be accounted for by mean reversion alone, with dire consequences for their shareholders. Ulrike Malmendier, the same behavioral economist who studied CEO overconfidence, has done the math: CEOs who win big awards from business magazines, such as "Best Performing CEO" (*Forbes*) or "Best Manager" (*Business Week*) do appear to be jinxed. The stocks of their companies declined an average of 60% over the next few years. For good measure, Malmendier looked at successful CEOs who could have been a contender for superstar status, but failed to win the actual award. The stocks of their companies declined, too, but not as much, only 45% on average. It is also worth pointing out that as their company's performance suffered and shareholder value was destroyed, superstar CEOs got raises, with a jump in pay to match their new public status.

It is hard to disentangle why exactly superstar CEOs stumble so badly once they hit star status. Maybe they believe their own press, and at some point morph from a human to a brand, always a mistake. Malmendier offers another possibility: They get distracted. Once they reach superstar status, the CEOs have a lot of other claims on their time than running their business. There are more press interviews and talk shows, keynote speeches around the globe, plus the opportunity to serve on the board of lots of prestigious organizations. And then there is golf. The golf handicaps of superstar CEOs are excellent (14.29 compared to 15.46 for their nonsuperstar peers). Malmendier formally writes of her finding: "These cross-sectional patterns are consistent with powerful CEOs spending time on the golf course that shareholders would prefer them to spend on firm business."

Last but not least, superstar CEOs write books, lots of them, while still allegedly working as CEO. These are usually variations on the theme of "how I did it," but there are different subgenres at work: memoirs of a difficult childhood, overcoming adversity, how to fix the planet, and so on. Malmendier found superstar CEOs were three times more likely to write books than regular CEOs, and the more awards the CEO has received, the more books written. Al Dunlap, of Sunbeam fame, was in the middle of promoting his book *Mean Business: How I Save Bad Companies and Make Good Companies Great*, when he was fired. The timing of Martha Stewart's business book was even more embarrassing. She achieved her success in part as an author but she departed from her usual food display advice to offer business tips in *The Martha Rules: 10 Essentials for Achieving Success as You Start, Grow, or Manage a Business*. The book was released the same year Stewart was released from prison. My rule: Next time you see a business bestseller by a CEO who is still working, read it if you like but by all means sell the stock.

30

Firing CEOs

All good things must come to end. And this is true for being a CEO as well. Circumstances vary, but forced terminations of CEOs show certain patterns and common factors regardless of the individual and individual company. Even though some CEOs had it coming, others are fired for factors beyond their control, while still others should be fired but aren't.

The dark science of studying CEO firings is the special focus of Dirk Jenter, a finance professor at Stanford. Some of what he has discovered is not surprising: CEOs are more likely to be fired in bad times than good. And many of these firings make sense. When the economy overall is performing poorly, the CEOs of companies that are doing particularly badly and scraping the bottom of their industry are the ones most likely to be fired.

But what about the flipside, when the economy is doing well? Jenter has found CEOs are very unlikely to be terminated during these boom times, and this holds true for the worst performing CEOs during this period as well. A rising tide seems to lift all boats. But clearly, this isn't fair or ideal. Rationally, it seems companies could still improve their performance by firing CEOs who are just floating up with the tide, rather than excelling. They aren't exactly "exceeding expectations" to use the HR term, and they are still getting paid a lot.

Therefore, it is actually the "not firing" of CEOs that really is most puzzling, and also unfair. If the industry overall is doing well, but their companies in particular are doing relatively poorly, why are so many underperforming CEOs kept onboard?

One reason has to do with the way corporate boards work. Jenter explained to me that operationally, it is very difficult for a board to fire a CEO during good times: "If thing are going reasonable well, and the firm is growing but up only 15%, whereas everyone else is up 20%, that still isn't a crisis. Internal dynamics make it difficult to justify confronting and firing a CEO without some sort of crisis with the stock really down," says Jenter.

Corporate boards and investors might also be tripped up by intuition. We don't intuitively distinguish between whether the rising stock price is being driven upward by the CEO alone, or just the broader market. Perceptions tells us the stock is still up, whereas formal analysis would show everyone else's stock is up more and shareholders could benefit from a new CEO. During boom years, CEOs who should otherwise be fired are happy to exploit both this lack of crisis and the misperception about their performance. Instead of waiting for the tide to turn and an actual crisis to get rid of bad CEOs, here is another idea from Jenter: "Even in good times, a corporate board still needs to rock the boat."

31

Using CEO Behavior for Investing

Warren Buffett once said, "The best CEOs love operating their companies and don't prefer going to Business Round Table meetings or playing golf at Augusta National." Investors should identify companies with this sort of CEO as opposed to ones where the CEOs write a lot of books proclaiming how great they are. Alternatively, investors can short the stock of companies where the CEOs are obviously flawed. The warning signs are the CEOs who are making too many acquisitions, are spending time on the book (and golf) circuit rather than at their desks, and finally are holding way too many options until expiration, indicating they are overconfident to the point of not being prudent with their own finances. Ulrike Malmendier suggests that concerned investors should show up at the annual meeting and make sure the superstar CEO doesn't get all that he or she wants: The message to the CEO is performance matters, not status. It is also clear the good corporate governance (which sounds more boring than it is) is crucial. Good governance is typically associated with lots of outside board members rather than just cronies of the CEO as well as the presence of large institutional shareholders. The quality matters because well-governed firms can keep a check on superstar CEOs, making sure they stay focused on the company. They can also exert pressure on underperforming CEOs in boom markets and cut them less slack. The main message is the board needs to hire the right sort of CEO for the company in the first place, because CEOs, in good times and bad, are inflexible in their individual strategies and find it hard to adapt.

At a deeper level, this analysis of CEOs shows the limits of trying to fix behavior through financial incentives alone. Although this insight seems strange coming out of economics, it is clear that there is more going on in our decisions than simple economic motives. The traditional remedy for potential CEO and other executive failures is to "align incentives." The idea is that if CEOs are rewarded when the company prospers, their inherent greed—and rationality—will drive them to make the right choice, increasing their pay and the stock price alike. They don't have to put themselves *or* the company first: Aligning incentives is the recipe for a win-win. This simplistic notion is now unchallenged in corporate life, and has rapidly spread to other sectors such as healthcare. The thinking is that the primary motive behind most actions is the profit motive. In boiled-down form, economic determinism explains everything: Just follow the money.

But life is more complicated than this, and so is human behavior, as the performance of CEOs shows. If you aren't sure what the right behavior is, then paying people more to do what they *think* is the right thing isn't going to solve anything. Overconfident CEOs already believe they are maximizing shareholder value and their own value by undertaking lots of acquisitions. Inflexible CEOs who have the wrong "style" for a particular situation (such as being a cost cutter) will work even harder to implement this damaging strategy if given strong pay incentives because this is what they truly believe in, this is what they think works.

32

Wall Street CEOs

In the end, hubris, the greatest sin in the Greek world, may explain more about Wall Street CEO behavior than simple greed. Other pathologies common to CEOs, such as superstar status and inflexibility, played roles as well. The demise of the CEOs of Wall Street resembles nothing so much as the calamities in a Greek tragedy. The CEOs, with their vast reputations and gravity-defying or really God-defying pay packages, couldn't imagine the end was coming.

Aligned or misaligned incentives seem really beside the point to describe CEO behavior during the final days of the crisis. Take the case of James Cayne, the former CEO of Bear Stearns. He had every economic as well as personal motive for Bear Stearns to succeed. Traders working for Cayne may have had an incentive to hit and run, to go for broke in their trades. If their trading strategy worked out, they got a huge bonus. If it didn't, the traders could hit the company with the loss and just look for a new job. This "tails I win, heads you lose" scenario wasn't true of Cayne himself: He was closely tied to the company, and his stake in Bear Stearns was immense. At one point he was worth a billion dollars and ranked 384 in the *Forbes* 400 wealthy Americans. After the collapse, this was reduced to a mere $61 million, but he really needed this money—he had just purchased a $20-million apartment in New York's former Plaza Hotel.

Despite having "skin in the game" (another corporate buzzword for having money at stake), Cayne seemed curiously hands-off during the crisis. He continued to play bridge and golf throughout, taking a helicopter each Thursday afternoon to his favorite golf club in New Jersey. Although he at one point traveled to China to try to find financing to save Bear, he was actually at a bridge tournament in Detroit the day clients began to desert the company en masse. (Cayne later revealed his health problems may have accounted for some of his behavior—he had recently been hospitalized for a serious prostate infection.) Cayne did not avoid blame for Bear's collapse, saying to *Fortune* magazine, "I didn't stop it, I didn't rein in the leverage," adding, "When you become road kill, when...you're not really healthy, but you know one thing—you know that you have worked your ass off and you're not smart enough to know the answer—that's tough."

Richard Fuld of Lehman Brothers is an even clearer example of a CEO's overconfidence leading his company to ruin. Of all the troubled New York investment banks, Lehman was the only one to actually go bankrupt. "The fall of Lehman isn't a story of greed, it's about Dick and his hubris," says of one Fuld's former Lehman lieutenants, who adds, "Dick thought the company was worth more than any of the suitors were offering. He never thought Lehman would go down. He never thought he was betting the ranch. He never thought he was putting the company at risk. This simply didn't come into his mind."

Fuld's financial interests were aligned with his company's. The bulk of his compensation was in stock. As an individual, he was the single largest owner of Lehman shares. He was in this sense betting his own money on the firm's fortunes. Under Fuld's reign, Lehman made vast profits on mortgages, both residential as well as commercial. The company acted as if it never believed the music could ever stop. Internal PowerPoint presentations forecast housing prices only going up. Lehman bought into its own forecasts and actually bought companies making subprime mortgages. In 2004, it acquired BNC, a top subprime mortgage lender, which it was forced to close three years later.

Where was Fuld in all of this? Ringing up the cash register, and remaining supremely confident, actually overconfident. Here is a typical story about his personality, from a trader: "Dick was unbelievably certain of his own view. He pushed his own market instincts first where they pertained to market direction. An example would be talking about buying or selling complex securities. He didn't focus on how good the idea was, he had a view of where the market was going." Traders had to follow his viewpoint. Moreover this particular trader isn't certain that Fuld fully understood the complex strategy on offer. Instead, that day Fuld liked Treasuries and so the trader had to make a straightforward bet on Treasuries.

At the Lehman alumni reception in the Spring of 2008, when the company was beginning to show signs of trouble, Fuld was as arrogant as ever, thanking the ex-employees for their help yet implying the company was better off without them. A Lehman alum remembers, "It was vintage Dick. Dick was being a dick."

These stories could be dismissed as sour grapes. After all, employees have every reason to be bitter. Lehman's emphasis on aligning incentives by encouraging employees to keep their compensation in company stocks, and sometimes forcing them to do so, meant that when the company went under, executives lost fortunes.

But understanding Fuld, his personality, and his overconfidence is crucial to explaining what happened at Lehman during its final months in existence and ultimate death spiral. Fuld was slow to react to the most ominous warning signs about the credit market, such as the collapse of Bear. Lehman had a huge number of loans on mortgages but chose not to take a loss. The company remained overconfident it was insulated from the worst risks and apparently not aware of how exposed Lehman truly was.

By mid-June of 2008, the Treasury department pressured Lehman to find a buyer. Lehman wouldn't or couldn't. The Treasury itself refused to guarantee to protect two potential suitors, Barclay's and Bank of America, from Lehman losses if they acquired the company, scuppering those deals. But Lehman was still being courted by the Korean Development Bank (KDB). As late as September 2008, with the end of Lehman near, the KDB President said, "It is difficult to predict the outcome of negotiations with Lehman Brothers due to differences over price."

Here is how someone in the Lehman camp (who wasn't directly involved in the negotiations) views Fuld's actions: "Corporate arrogance did him in, in the end. The arrogance was he had the Koreans who were going to invest in the company and he could have said yes, but he was sure his company was worth more. There was a fundamental disagreement in value. Lehman was soon worth nothing. But he never believed the government would let Lehman fail."

The Korean deal fell through. Fuld also overestimated his political capital. The U.S. Government had rescued Bear and Fannie and Freddie, so it was easy to see why Fuld was confident the government would rescue Lehman as a last resort. But Fuld, the consummate trader, bet wrong. The day the company went bankrupt, the signs outside Lehman Brothers New York corporate headquarters read, "Great trade, Dick."

After Lehman collapsed, the dominos started to fall. The stock market crashed. Merrill Lynch could have been the next investment bank to go under, but its new CEO John Thain was able to prevent this from happening. For years Merrill had been playing catch-up with Lehman in mortgage-backed securities and explicitly followed Lehman's playbook. It bought a subprime lender in the U.S., First Franklin, as well a loan servicing company in Europe. By 2006, the strategy paid off: Merrill was the largest CDO (collateralized debt obligation) underwriter in the world. It retained many CDOs on its books. By 2007, Merrill was a mess. The CEO, E. Stanley O'Neal, was fired and awarded $161 million to leave.

John Thain, the new CEO, had arrived from the New York Stock Exchange. He didn't follow Lehman's playbook. He sold off bad assets as quickly as he was able to and wrote off the rest. When it was clear the company was unlikely to be saved by these actions, he made the decision to sell Merrill Lynch itself. The deal with Bank of America was reached on a Sunday, Sept 14th, less than 24 hours *before* Lehman went under.

I don't know if Thain's expedient actions came about because he was less overconfident than the two other CEOs. He showed signs of grandiosity at his next job at Bank of America. Thain spent a million dollars on refurnishing his office, including $28,000 for curtains, $87,000 for a rug, and $1,400 on a trash can. And the takeover deal he had arranged proved disastrous from Bank of America's perspective, but at least it stopped Merrill from disappearing into oblivion, salvaging some value for the company.

I think one reason he was able to reach a takeover deal, unlike Fuld, is that Thain didn't have the same emotional investment in Merrill Lynch that Fuld had in Lehman Brother or James Cayne had in Bear Stearns. They had built their entire careers at their firms. Thain, in contrast, was new and was hired to fix a very damaged company. Free from the emotional attachment and baggage of a lifetime at the company, Thain made the nonsentimental choice and simply sold Merrill Lynch.

◆ ◆ ◆

In October of 2008, Richard Fuld was called in to testify before Congress about the demise of Lehman Brothers. His testimony concluded with a typically high-handed statement: "I am available to answer any questions you may have." (Where else did he have to go? At this point there wasn't much standing between him and jail.)

But during the testimony and in his response to questions, Fuld repeated over and over, almost like a refrain, that his incentives were aligned. "The interests of the executives and the employees were aligned," said Fuld. "My long-term financial interests were completely aligned with those of all the other shareholders. No one had more incentives to see Lehman Brothers succeed." This is undeniably true. But it just wasn't enough.

◆ ◆ ◆

In the next part of this book, I turn to the credit crisis and the role bank CEOs and many, many other players had in creating it. Greed may explain some of the crisis, but as the examples of Dick Fuld and James Cayne show, simple economic motives alone don't explain everything. Psychological factors were at work as well. Markets and market participants weren't acting fully rationally. I examine different aspects of the overall crisis and the bubbles that led up to it through a behavioral economics prism.

Part V
Psychology and the Credit Crisis

This is the way the world ends, not with a bang but a whimper.

—T. S. Eliot

This is the way the world ends, not with a whim but a banker.

—Jazz musician Paul Desmond

33

Background: Bubbles and When They Explode

Financial bubbles—like soap bubbles—have their own predictable features. They share a common disturbed architecture with easily identifiable, if unstable, contours. Their origins are often murky, but a rise in price attracts the interest of investors who push prices still higher, creating the belief that price can only go up and up, until they eventually reach unsustainable levels culminating in a pop and a messy aftermath with a lot of financial debris scattered on the ground.

Financial bubbles can be easily created and replicated in experimental economics laboratories. Economics, much like psychology, now uses experiments to test and analyze basic principles. In these experiments, groups of traders participate in laboratory-created markets, buying and selling financial assets. The course of their trading helps economists understand how markets work. Laws of supply and demand and their impact on price can be identified and predicted with near perfect accuracy and clarity. And, under very specific conditions, bubbles can arise, giving new insight into both their birth and final moments before their explosive demise.

Charlie Plott is an experimental economist at Caltech who creates and analyzes financial bubbles. Plott was raised in Oklahoma and comes from a distinguished Southern family; the Plott Hound, the official dog of North Carolina, was named after an ancestor. Plott has a bracing, unpretentious country charm, rare in economics, which belies the sophistication of his research. His lab consists of computer-linked trading screens. During the experiment, traders buy and sell assets. With sweat forming on their brows, they look like pros, although they actually tend to be undergraduates. Participants are motivated by the opportunity to make real money. The amounts are sufficient "to give participants a shot of adrenaline if they do well," as Plott puts it, or alternatively kick themselves if they lose it all and leave empty-handed. Real financial incentives are known to be important for creating proper experimental control. Plott analyzes the course of the market action, mapping the price changes that result.

Plott explains to me what he has learned from his lab: "The way information is conveyed through markets is through 'bids' and 'asks.' (The bid is the price someone is willing to pay and the ask is the price someone is willing to sell.) When you have insiders with good news, they compete with each other for exposure to the market. They do this by increasing their bid and getting inside the bid-ask spread. If someone is in front of me, the only way I can get in front of them and get exposure to this market is to bid a higher price. If the best bid is 100, I will then go to 101."

These traders with inside knowledge of good news bid fiercely against each other to get in "the front of the book," and prices begin to rise. This carries information to the rest of the market, including outsiders who don't have first-hand inside information on the good news. Expectations get built up. People see a rising market and start piling on top. A cascade of bidding occurs. The price shoots up.

This isn't a bubble.

As Plott explains, "This cascade, or 'herding behavior' as it is sometimes called, is almost always correct." Insiders have real good news or other information they are trading on, and they are aggressive about it. In another words, the new price reflects changed fundamentals. The information about this change spreads throughout the market from the results of traders' actions. The market is merely reacting to and finally incorporating the good news.

A bubble is different. Says Plott, "In a bubble the wrong guys get in the market first, but no real new information is out there." This time there is no new "good news," but people are trading anyway. These traders start giving off the wrong signals. The market thinks they know something but they don't, and prices swoop off course. Says Plott, "The anatomy of this type of bubble is well understood. The process itself has to do with coordination and miscues and is quite understandable from a classic point of view."

The anatomy of a bubble in its late, decadent stage, just before it is going to pop, has its own unique features. The market starts giving signals there is a problem, according to Plott, most noticeably in an asymmetry between buy and sell orders. Before, it was rational to keep buying because there was always someone else who would pay you more for it later, but people begin to realize aside from this they have no inside information. That is, buyers are losing confidence, and they start looking to the market itself for answers. And the market isn't reinforcing any good news. Buyers start leaving the market. Those who are left are frightened and send in very low bids. The discrepancy between asking price and selling price widens and then becomes unstable. Finally, the bubble pops.

"This can easily be seen in restaurants as well," says Plott. When you are deciding which restaurant to go to, one way to choose is to look around for the one with the most people. This is typically a good signal. But you have to assume the other diners know something and share your tastes. Says Plott, "This is how information aggregates. You observe behavior and act on it, but you are making assumptions that other people are rational."

A bubble, in contrast, is like a bad restaurant that keeps drawing a crowd—because it keeps drawing a crowd—until someone finally admits how terrible the food is. The crowd is watching each other thinking someone else must know something, but no one knows anything. The only one in on the game is the restaurant, which has somehow figured out ways to keep the restaurant full. "This is why some restaurants offer a free bottle of wine for early diners, to get them to come sit in their restaurant," says Plott. "The restaurant places them in the window where other people can see them. You assume people sitting there know something, and use them as a cue to go into the restaurant. That is a bubble."

In addition to seeing bubbles in action, you can sometimes *hear* them. In the days before electronic trading, stock markets used to have characteristic sounds, with the volume ratcheting up as trading became frenzied. Plott has been able to convey the sound of a stock market bubble by selecting sounds to accompany the bids and asks in his lab experiments. Each different price is a different note on a scale, making a pinging sound as traders place orders. A high sound is a high bid or ask, and a low sound is a low bid or ask. As the bubble becomes less of sure thing, the sound changes. The low notes, representing low bids, become more frequent. The sounds become less stable with ominous intervals. The end is near. (If you want to listen to the sound of a market bubble, and hear it telling you things, Plott's experiment can be found at http://eeps.caltech.edu/mov/sound_of_market.html).

Neoclassical economists argue that although bubbles can easily be created in economic labs, and maybe in the restaurant industry, the same can't be said for financial markets, incredible as this sounds. They argue that financial bubbles are the exception, not the norm, regardless of the evidence provided by the credit and real-estate bubbles, the tech bubble, and the Roaring '20s, to say nothing of the Dutch tulip bubble.

The transfer of information from one person to another through the market is technically known as "information aggregation." The mainstream economics point of view is that because it constantly works so well, and because it creates so much value while working, the instances of aggregation failure (misaggregation) attract much attention. Often people are lead to believe that the common mode for markets is aggregation failure when, in fact, the mode is aggregation success. Competitive markets always include irrational participants;

this is factored in; they don't usually throw the market off course. If anything, markets tend toward stable equilibrium, in the same way hurricanes are not an everyday experience, or passenger jets tend to be stable while aloft. There have to be several factors at work to create a bubble, a complex misalignment hard to capture in a simple experiment.

Although lab bubbles have certain identifiable features, I asked Plott if this makes it easier to forecast the bursting of bubbles in the real world. He pointed out that part of the challenge is economists rarely agree that a bubble even exists, making it even harder to spot a looming "pop." For instance, a convincing argument could still be made (and one I don't agree with) that the rise in U.S. real estate prices wasn't a bubble characterized by speculation but was instead a rational response to easy credit.

In terms of spotting bubbles and predicting their demise, Plott himself warns, "You need to be careful. We still don't understand everything about financial markets. These are big and complex systems. We know many of the clues from the science, but that does not guarantee that we will be able to solve the crime." There is one central lesson investors can still draw from these experiments, and that is to question themselves why they are trading. Is it based on real information and good news where the investor knows something? And if not, do the people investors are turning to for guidance know something? Anything?

What is clear is few investors were asking themselves these questions in the months before the crash. And by late 2008, the U.S. and global financial markets were no longer operating smoothly. The supposed stability assumed by neoclassical economics was in scant evidence. The U.S. financial industry and financial markets had broken down. The Western world's banking system seemed to be coming to an end.

In the years leading up to the panic, the world had been caught up in a series of interconnected financial illusions, operating on many different levels with many different participants. At the heart of one was the mania of real-estate investors who were certain they could just keep flipping houses forever. But the financial services industry experienced its own mania as well in the form of the credit bubble. The industry tried to exploit real-estate investors before finally succumbing to a comparable irrational frenzy. Finally, regulators played their own special role as enablers or worse, refusing to "lean against the wind" of the growing manias. Both real-estate investors and the investment banks were allowed to use leverage almost without limit to their hearts content. As Federal Reserve Chairman Alan Greenspan was later to admit, he was in the grip of his own illusion that rational self-interest would protect everyone involved from their own worst instincts.

Let us now turn to the case of a real-estate investor and see how his supposed rational self-interest guided his investments in the overheated real-estate market of South Florida. His actions are right out of one of Plott's lab experiments: He kept buying houses confident he could flip them to someone for more money later, only to realize he had no inside market information and the market he had turned to for guidance was about to trap him.

34

Fear and Loathing in Ft. Lauderdale

The subprime market dislocation widely discussed in the months leading up to the full-blown financial panic of Autumn 2008 was not an abstract or faraway concept in South Florida in the spring of that year. In Ft. Lauderdale, as soon as you exited the freeway it was clear there was a problem: a tattered sign next to the off-ramp begged "Investors needed: properties offered at 50% of assessed value." This was merely a hint of what was to come. Off Las Olas Boulevard, the city's main drag, things seemed to get worse, not better. Every house and condo on the glittering waterfront streets seemed to have the exact same yellowing, faded sign: "For Sale." The mortgage broker's office was closed and had its own "For Rent" sign. Even a church was for sale.

The downtown of the city consisted of large, often empty condominium towers. The growing number of unoccupied and foreclosed apartments increased the carrying charges and hurricane insurance for the few buyers left in the buildings, making mortgage defaults more likely. In every direction you looked, more condos were under construction. To the south was a forest of construction cranes: dismal Hollywood, Florida, best known for being home to the 9/11 terrorists and the place where Anna Nicole Smith died. And in the far distance was an even larger clump of condos: Miami.

At the center of downtown Ft. Lauderdale, at the base of the luxury towers and facing the river is the city's landmark: the Stranahan House. This little white structure was built as a trading post in 1901 by Ft. Lauderdale pioneer Frank Stranahan. As every Ft. Lauderdale city guidebook will tell you, here he traded with Seminole Indians, ran the post office, and oversaw the first town hall. What the city fathers don't like to emphasize is that Stranahan was a suicide: He drowned himself in the river in front during the Great Depression.

South Florida real estate has a history of boom and bust, a manic-depressive economy if you will. The "market downturn"—a polite euphemism for mass panic—was in direct proportion to the excessive optimism in evidence only a few months before. Then buyers would camp outside new condos overnight in order to get in on the real-estate action. Whereas now the market was driven by fear, then it was driven by another emotion—greed. Fear and greed are two sides of the same coin. They are present not just in South Florida real-estate markets, but in ourselves.

Mathew's story is one of human resilience, as well as of overconfidence, a widespread human bias. "Overconfidence" can describe many beliefs and thoughts but, for behavioral economists, it usually has a much narrower and more precise meaning: an investor's belief that past trends will continue in the future. For example, Mathew was "overconfident" that housing prices would just keep rising. But in his case, the usual, broader definition of "overconfident" describes very well Matthew's personality.

His story is also about something else—the changing regulatory as well as mortgage industry policies that made it all too easy for Mathew to indulge his overconfidence and appetite for risk. If Matthew had tried to buy stocks on margin to the degree he used leverage in his real-estate investments, he would have found it was illegal. The Federal Reserve has margin requirements that strictly limit the amount of stock that can bought on credit. According to Fed regulations, the maximum loan value for margin stock is 50%. This was set in 1974 and has been static since then. Prior to this, since 1934, the Fed would raise and lower margin requirements in response to market conditions, using it as a tool to dampen speculation in overheated markets. At least when it comes to regulating stocks, the Fed apparently has never forgotten the 1929 crash and the role margin calls may have played.

I was in Ft. Lauderdale to interview a homeowner who had participated in the market boom, to learn more about the mindset during the mania. Broward County (Ft. Lauderdale) and Dade County (Miami) along with Las Vegas and Phoenix were at the center of the U.S. subprime speculative boom.

"Matthew" as he asked to be called (I have changed his name and other identifying details from our discussion, although not the content of our conversation) could only talk with me in between his frequent visits to his church. Like many, he had become devoutly religious since the crash. James Cayne, the former CEO of Bear Stearns, also sought solace and answers in religion after losing $900 million when his company collapsed.

Matthew's home was in an older, "classic" country club community west of Ft. Lauderdale. There was no security gate. I just drove straight in, through winding roads of houses with For Sale signs. Some houses had well-maintained yards, others were going to seed. Matthew's was singular: His house was surrounded by a 20-foot-high fichus hedge. Mathew was in the backyard, lounging by the pool and the outdoor kitchen. He was about 55 years old. He was neither friendly nor unfriendly. His first words to me were that his backyard was big enough to take a 60-yard golf shot. I think the point was two-fold: He had a big yard, but also he didn't need to belong to a country club, which, as he later revealed, he could no longer afford in any case. Settling back into his lounge chair in the Florida sun, he told me about his investments, a story shared by many in town:

> "I flipped 45 properties in total. The properties were one-and-a-half acres or larger, American dream houses, 2,500 to 7,000 square feet. I called my business 'farming.' All the houses were close to me. I could fall out of bed and get to the houses in a few minutes. I could turn them around in as little as two months. And I could make six figures on a house."

Originally, Matthew co-owned the houses with partners. "I used other people's money. But then I went it alone. I just used mine." By mine, Matthew is referring to mortgages he obtained from banks. The entire operation was based on this leverage: "I put it on mortgages. I would put up 20% and the bank would put up the rest."

His wife warned him he was getting in over his head, to "take some money off the table," Mathew reports. "I said having a house is as good as money in the bank. And I'm good at catching curves. The ride was going great."

Not only did investors believe prices could only go up, they were told in the newspaper each day that the population in South Florida could also only go up as the baby boomers retired, creating pressure for higher real-estate prices. In fact, once the crisis hit, the populations of Broward and Dade began to dip.

The real-estate market began to slip into reverse as early as 2005. Matthew at this point owned 12 houses. He was able to sell 5. He was stuck with the remaining 7. The banks still have these mortgages on their balance sheets.

Says Matthew, matter-of-factly, "Look, it was a run and then it was a washout. To give you an idea, I haven't paid the mortgage of my own house for 18 months. The bank hasn't come after me."

Matthew therefore hasn't technically defaulted. He is merely "delinquent." The bank hasn't foreclosed. Nor has he declared bankruptcy—his wife has a job and supports them. (She was at work the weekend I interviewed him; he wouldn't say where.) They no longer belong to the country club, but they still play golf—at a public course for $14 a round. Matthew doesn't have a credit card because he doesn't want to stick someone else with the bill if he has to declare bankruptcy: "I'm very religious," he points out.

He adds: "I wouldn't give a person a bad deal if I knew it was a bad deal. I made money for a lot of people. Nobody got beat for a nickel dealing with me, except now the banks of course. The banks are writing off their balance sheets. I would like to pay, but I don't have the cash to do this. I have no problem owing money to the banks. They thought I was good enough to lend it to. They thought I was a good risk. I thought I was a good risk. And then the markets turned down."

I notice the pool is cloudy. He is no longer maintaining it and cannot swim in it.

Matthew tells me: "I'll do it again. I've been a millionaire more than once. I've lost it more than once. I've landed on my feet before. I don't know how the market will turn out. Maybe I'll be blessed."

When it comes to using leverage for real estate, the door is wide open. Whereas you have to put 50% down for buying stocks, for houses you can put 0% down. However, in the past, banks would, of course, only loan money to people they were certain could repay them. But in the bubble years this was no longer the case.

One change was the Community Reinvestment Act (CRA) of 1977, which was enacted in response to concerns banks were denying credit to people in poor neighborhoods, a practice known as "redlining." The CRA outlawed such discrimination. The CRA remained an obscure and little used law until the Clinton administration began to reinterpret it, and actively enforce it. Banks were now required to demonstrate they were actively making mortgage loans to low-income people, the sort of borrowers who tended to have little savings, lots of debt, and spotty credit histories. Fannie Mae and Freddie Mac were required to buy many of these loans as part of their "affordable housing goals and subgoals." But this government intervention is only part of the picture and wouldn't apply to people like Matthew in any case. It certainly contributed to the loosening of mortgage lending standards, but the bigger story is there was a growing industry waiting to exploit this small opening. The mortgage industry had transformed itself into something unrecognizable. It no longer really cared about the credit quality of the borrowers it was lending to; in fact, it seemed to have no inhibitions at all. Its only concern was making new loans. The industry had convinced itself it had found a way to abolish risk: It had discovered a way to take an illiquid asset such as a mortgage, and through financial engineering, turn it into a tradable security, a process I look at next. The word for this modern version of alchemy is "securitization."

35

Follow the Mortgage

Before the late 1970s, most mortgages were the property—and responsibility—of the banks and Saving and Loans issuing them. This meant the banks had the strictest underwriting standards and were extremely careful about to whom they loaned money. The banks still faced dangers caused by homeowners' behavior, even solvent homeowners. The major risk was the possibility people might prepay their mortgage ahead of time; when interest rates fall, borrowers refinance their mortgage and pay up early. Although this seems like a bizarre and minor worry in light of today's risks of defaults and foreclosures, prepayment actually causes huge problems for banks. A bank may have thought it had a high-yielding loan, but prepayment ends this lucrative arrangement. The bank has its money back, but it now has to make new loans at a lower interest rate in a less profitable environment.

The securitization business is underpinned by the ratings agencies, such as Standard and Poor's, Fitch, or Moody's. These "agencies," all for-profit companies, were mostly in the business of ratings bonds and the companies issuing them, assigning them letter grades such as AAA or BB based on their creditworthiness. With the rise of bond-like structured products, the agencies expanded their business into rating these newer instruments. They simply used their expertise and techniques for analyzing bonds and applied them to mortgage-backed securities.

As Ranieri once said, "The whole creation of mortgage securities was involved with a rating." The rating lets investors of these artificially structured products know exactly what they are buying. Huge pension funds are often only legally allowed to invest in AAA-rated securities. Also, investors usually have lower capital charges or reserve requirements for highly rated assets. Alternatively, investors with a higher taste for risk and return could buy securities with a lower rating.

The banks creating the mortgage-backed securities were able to slice and dice them in different ways to create products with different ratings to serve these different markets. These different slices are known as different "tranches." Even if the overall pool of mortgage had a lot of problems such as high prepayment risk or default risk, the bank could slice off a top "tranche" with few risks, obtain an AAA rating for it, and sell it to an investor who wanted triple A. The middle slice, with medium risks and a lower rating, could be served up for investors with these tastes. The worst tranches were labeled "toxic waste."

The securitization model can get a lot more complicated very quickly, and it is already complex to begin with. The different tranches in turn can be combined into a new security, generically referred to as a collateralized debt obligation (CDO). And this, in turn, can be diced and sliced in numerous ways. Or different CDOs can be combined yet again, to form a CDOs squared. The issuer would usually take out insurance in case of default in the form of a credit default swap (CDS). And sometimes CDSs were, in turn, securitized and sold off to investors who wanted to speculate in creditworthiness. If you are confused by all the acronyms used in the securitization industry, think of how obscure these names were before the industry became front page news. I believe this confusion is intentional—deploying lots of acronyms is an old bureaucratic trick to keep outsiders in the dark.

Lou Ranieri was a college dropout who had previously aspired to be an Italian chef before ending up on the mortgage trading desk at Salomon Brothers. Ranieri had an insight that simultaneously solved the prepayment problem and could bring enormous profits to local banks and investment banks. His idea was that he could pool the mortgages together and issue bonds based on them. Just like diversifying your portfolio reduces total risk, pooling all the mortgages together diversified the banks' risks in case some homeowners prepaid. Ranieri called this process "securitization." He was creating new, tradeable financial securities out of any underlying asset that promised some sort of cash flow. For mortgages, the bond based on the underlying pool of mortgages was called, not surprisingly, a "mortgage-backed security."

For local banks, mortgage-backed securities had many advantages over holding individual mortgages: The bonds created out of the pools could be sold off to other investors. The local bank went from being the investor and also owner of the mortgage to simply being a company that originated and serviced the mortgage.

This last point was the true beauty of securitization. Before mortgage loan companies were limited by how many mortgages they were willing to keep on their balance sheet. Now this was no longer a concern. Securitization increased the banks' capacity to originate and service loans—which is where all the profit was—while simultaneously reducing their exposure to the asset class, namely mortgages. What ultimately happened to the mortgage of borrowers like Matthew was someone else's problem, the investor in the mortgage-backed security.

The securitization industry, pioneered by Ranieri at Salomon Brothers in the 1970s, was spectacularly lucrative. Michael Lewis' 1980s best seller *Liar's Poker* about life inside Wall Street describes the excesses as well as successes of Ranieri and the business of securitization. "Mortgages were so cheap your teeth hurts," was just one of Ranieri's usual sales pitches to investors in his securities. Although during the 2008 crisis mortgage-backed securities were often described as exotic and new, this clearly isn't entirely true.

Despite the complexity of the pooled mortgage-backed security, whatever name given to it, the investment theme is fairly simple. The security offers decent returns but also safety because it is based on pools of assets. The tranche structure and insurance add extra protection. The message from the investment banks is securitized products are so sophisticated and complex, so brilliantly financially engineered and carefully structured, with insurance and outside ratings adding extra layers of safety, that they had little to do with the small-time problems of small-time homeowners in Florida. But this was not the case.

♦ ♦ ♦

Structured products, consisting of mortgage-backed and similar securities, became America's single largest export during the twenty-first century. About $27 trillion were sold during this time, roughly double America's annual GDP. The business easily dwarfed movies or passenger airplanes or weapons systems, usually thought of America's main export industries.

This securitized system, despite its secure sounding name, had encountered several serious crises on its way up. The first serious one was in Southern California in the early '90s, when real estate in L.A. crashed. The likely cause was not the L.A. riots (the downturn started before them) but instead stemmed from the closing of U.S. military bases in the region as well as a recession. Thousands of homeowners defaulted. Companies insuring the mortgages were financially stressed. But the mortgage-backed securities were based on *national* pools of mortgages. Because there was no national downturn, but only a regional one, securitization worked, as it was supposed to. The pooling spread the risk. There was no need for structural change. The system held.

Then, in 1998, the hedge fund LTCM failed. The prices of many financial assets collapsed as well. But real estate was fine. Mortgage-backed securities, based on this solid asset, came out looking like a winner. There was a flight to quality, and this meant investors were buying up mortgage-backed securities.

By the early twenty-first century, it seemed like everyone wanted a piece of the mortgage-backed action: Chinese banks, European banks, hedge funds. The world was awash with liquidity and easy credit. The U.S. financial services industry was there to soak it up. China was saving close to half its GDP, and the money needed to be invested somewhere—and structured products were attractive, offering higher yields than U.S. treasuries. In the U.S., the Fed, under Chairman Alan Greenspan, maintained a "lax" interest rate policy. He reacted to the collapse of the dot-com bubble by lowering interest rates and keeping them there despite evidence of a new bubble in real estate. He argued, in his memorable phrase, that central banks could not "lean against the wind" of asset class bubbles. Much of this easy money flowed into real estate and ultimately into mortgage-backed securities.

The liquidity boom was also created by the process of securitization itself. As mortgage-backed securities rose in value, so did the assets of investment banks owning them (and most did). The highly leveraged banks, now with stronger balance sheets because the value of their assets had increased, could in turn take on much more business, including buying more mortgaged-backed securities, driving their prices in turn higher and increasing the value of the balance sheet yet again. This feedback loop, which is technically called an "amplification mechanism" by economists, looked like it could go on without end.

The reliability of the ratings issued by the ratings agency remained a weak point in this seemingly benign environment. The issuer (the New York investment banks) paid for the rating on their own security, not the buyer. Issuers could and did game the ratings agency system, seeking the most favorable ratings for their securities. If, say, one agency didn't like a transaction, then the issuer could just take it to someone else. Everyone was rating shopping. Of course, this meant the investment banks were therefore aware of the limitations and biases of the ratings they received, but the buyers of the securities were in no position to fully know this. However, the investment banks weren't as cunning as they thought. Despite their first hand knowledge of the agencies' practices, they relied heavily on ratings from the agencies for internal risk management, investments, and trades, and maintained heavy exposures to CDOs. Not everything was sold off to clueless foreign buyers.

Overall the role of the ratings agencies during the credit bubble was in some ways analogous to Wall Street stock analysts during the tech bubble. Both seemingly offered objective advice but really were mostly in the marketing business. Alan Greenspan, avoiding blaming himself for what happened next, instead pointed a finger at the agencies' practices in 2007: "People believed they knew what they were doing. And they didn't."

◆ ◆ ◆

"Securitization was an excellent business. For most of its life it worked very well. People forget that now." This is the opinion of Andrew Jones, a former lawyer who has spent virtually his entire career in the securitization industry. He started as a Wall Street attorney back in the 1980s at Cadwalader, Wickersham & Taft, one of the first law firms engaged in securitization. Later Jones became an executive at a ratings agency. (He prefers I don't say which one.) He describes life there during the final months of the securitization boom, before the crash:

> "The focus all over Wall Street was on getting the deals done.
> As the volume of so-called 'affordability loans' burgeoned,
> things began to get dicey, but the Street didn't want to recog-
> nize how bad the underwriting was."

What Jones is referring to is that by 2005 and 2006, mortgage brokers would lend money to almost anyone in order to feed the mortgage-backed security machine. This was the era when no-documentation mortgages and NINJA mortgages (no job verification, no income verification, no asset verification) become commonplace.

The psychological epicenter of the boom had shifted. Whereas the exuberance was at first most noticeable among real-estate speculators in places such as South Florida and Las Vegas, now the securitization system itself seemed gripped by mania. The system would do anything to generate more mortgages to securitize and sell off to investors, including foreign investors. Brokers were handing out copies of the movie Boiler Room (about "pump and dump" high-pressured stock sales practices) as a training tape to their loan officers. The loan officers had to watch the movie as their homework.

Mortgage borrowers now included larger and larger percentages of those classified as "subprime," meaning they were at high risk of default and had bad credit history. The market now felt that the rising price of the underlying assets—real estate—provided the ultimate insurance for the loan regardless of the credit problems of the borrower. But if prices were to fall or even flatten, the buyers of bundled mortgages were on the hook, not the local mortgage broker. The ratings agencies should have been significantly increasing the level of protection required on the securitization transactions—first, because of declining borrower quality and, second, because the higher prices rose, the more likely they were to fall. The rating agencies didn't.

The United States had not experienced a national, as opposed to regional, residential real-estate downturn since the depression. The pooled securities combined mortgages from across the nation so, as the quantitative models assumed, this risk was diversified away. The sophisticated models did not fully consider this possibility. Even AAA levels, if this disaster did occur, would have to be downgraded to junk level. And the lower tranches could actually default.

Says Jones, "Everyone was comfortable with these standards." Everyone had structures that worked as long as things didn't blow up in real estate. A national real-estate downturn was unthinkable. It was too remote. No one was ever protected to that level.

These problems were magnified as mortgage-backed securities were resecuritized in CDOs. CDOs were originally backed by only corporate bonds. When mortgage securities started to back CDOs in the late 1990s, says Jones, "The CDO groups at the agencies continued to look at the mortgage bonds as if they were corporate bonds. They thought a AAA-rated structured product was like a AAA-rated corporate bond. But that doesn't work. If you have lots of different corporate bonds, you are well diversified in case of a default. If you have lots of mortgage-backed securities, it only looks like you are well diversified."

The difference is that corporate bonds have much less systemic risk than structured products. When a producer of playing cards defaults, that doesn't imply a sneaker manufacturer will, too. A cupcake producer can go down, but a fire engine manufacture could be left standing. The pattern of corporate defaults is widely dispersed. Therefore, a portfolio combining bonds from very different companies in different industries should have an overall lower risk of defaults than owning them individually.

Similarly, the securitization industry believed that if you pool mortgages from, say, the Southeast and the Northeast, the regional nature of a real-estate downturn should have provided an analogous type of safety. But if homeowners defaulted from across the whole nation, then fundamentally you weren't diversified at all. Mortgage-backed securities can all move together. When prices began to fall toward the end of the credit boom, this is exactly what happened. Falling home prices revealed the real credit quality of borrowers. And they all began to default in a similar pattern, bringing down the mortgage-backed securities with them. The agencies, with their corporate-inspired CDO models, were not prepared for this. Their models didn't fully distinguish the likely co-movement of mortgaged-back bonds from the default pattern of corporate bonds.

In the late 1990s, Jones publicly objected to the development of CDOs backed by mortgages. In 2000, he stopped rating mortgages believing that the market was already getting frothy, frivolous, and uncertain. Jones has since left Wall Street and is now a nationally recognized cityscape painter. He has a social-psychological explanation of why Wall Street failed to heed alarms about the potential for systemic defaults. Says Jones, "Wall Street doesn't like naysayers. If you say, 'I don't think those deals will work,' then you are not a team player and you are making yourself redundant and obsolete. This is a harsh comment but a true one."

♦ ♦ ♦

U.S. home prices peaked in the second quarter of 2006. The initial decline following this high was almost imperceptibly small, hardly a bump, let alone a jolt. The S&P/Case-Shiller Home Price Index tracking changes in the residential housing market showed a decline in the third quarter of that year of .0095, less than 1%, too small for anyone to notice. Ominously, the downturn was *national.* Nonetheless, the securitization industry, whose models never considered a national downturn, didn't react. On a local level things were much worse. Matthew, the real estate speculator in Ft. Lauderdale had been unable to flip his houses since 2005, when the market there reversed.

An increase in defaults of subprime mortgages was picked up by several tracking indexes in the Spring of 2007. Behavioral economist Robert Shiller, co-founder of the index with his name, speaking at a conference in New York warned that real estate can go down as well as up, even in hot markets such as Los Angeles. I remember less about the presentation than I do the reaction of the audience. People afterward termed Shiller's speech "fantasies of a chronic depressive" and a "symptom of Shiller's mental state."

There were a handful of other Cassandra types, including IMF economist Raghuram Rajan, Dean Baker, and, interestingly, Lou Ranieri himself, the father of the securitization. In March 2007, he told *The Wall Street Journal* the problems in subprime were "the leading edge of the storm," adding, "We're not really sure what the guy's income is and...we're not sure what the house is worth.... So you can understand why some of us become a little nervous."

Nonetheless, the voices of doom were rare. The real-estate downturn was gentle, at least initially. Most economic forecasters were worried about a potential crisis in the dollar as well as America's unsustainable trade deficit. Similarly the bond market seemed blissfully calm, almost eerily so. The spreads between corporate bonds and treasuries were at historic lows, implying little credit risk. It took a great deal of mental ingenuity to read this as a sign of problems to come, but credit moves in cycles. Some bond managers I spoke to at the time saw that market as being so richly valued that a grim day of reckoning had to be in the offing. But no one knew what exactly the catalyst would be to pierce the credit bubble.

◆ ◆ ◆

"If you have something that is fundamentally hard to value, whose value is only determined by complex assumptions, once you leverage it, a little flaw becomes a fatal flaw. Through leverage, CDOs were turned into a dangerous, sharp, knife." This is how Nobel Laureate Harry Markowitz described to me the instrument that would ultimately pop the bubble.

Markowitz acknowledged to me that he, like most observers, didn't realize just how dangerous this "knife" had become. A single mortgage could be leveraged by a factor of 100. What was becoming increasingly clear, by the summer of 2007, is that mortgage-backed securities, which had been sold to banks, hedge funds, and pension plans across the world, were revealed to be quite different from what the ratings agencies and investment banks had promised. Some of the first problems to surface were outside of the U.S. IKB, a small German bank, had to be rescued by government intervention because of losses on its mortgage-backed securities. BNP Paribas in France froze redemptions from three funds, blaming its inability to adequately price U.S. structured products. In the U.S., New Century Financial, a subprime lender, declared bankruptcy in April; it was shortly followed by American Home Mortgage, which had targeted borrowers with good credit. Bear Stearns spent $3.2 billion bailing out its own hedge funds, which were caught up in the growing subprime problem. Quantitative hedge funds were running into difficulties as well. But the problems at this point seemed to be contained and did not appear to be systemic. What was not understood, until later, was the essential fragility of the structured finance system and how levered it was.

36

Risky Business: Bank Runs

In September of 2007, investors trying to access their accounts online at Northern Rock, a U.K. building society, found the website kept crashing. It was impossible to withdraw funds electronically. Investors were already anxious about the solvency of the bank because of its exposure to U.S. subprime mortgage-backed securities. Unable to withdraw funds any other way, customers began lining up outside Northern Rock branches at 3:00 a.m., waiting for the bank to open. Once they got inside, many refused to leave until they got their money. A couple in Cheltenham barricaded themselves and the local branch manager in her office until she would transfer their £1 million online account out of the bank. Eventually, police rescued the banker. Northern Rock was in the middle of a bank run, the first one in the U.K. in over 100 years, something that wasn't supposed to happen in an advanced Western society.

When someone shouts fire in a theater, the first ones out are the ones mostly to get out alive, even if the disorderly rush causes more deaths than an orderly evacuation. Similarly, "In a classic bank run—such as the one on Northern Rock—everybody has an incentive to be first at the bank teller or the first on the bank's Web site," notes Princeton economist Markus Brunnermeier. "People who withdraw their money early get their full amount, while those who move late might not."

Brunnermeier studies banks' liquidity problems in particular and financial bubbles in general. Although the underlying bubble may have been caused by psychologically driven investment manias, the unwinding could be coldly rational, with many victims caught in the vise of a financial system that had become illiquid. The panic that gripped the financial system during 2008 was all too warranted. It was just the popping of the real-estate and credit balloons inflated by investors' emotions, with the financial system finally falling back to earth. Bank runs were a rational response to this situation.

It is Brunnermeier's contention, in boiled-down form, that much of what occurred on Wall Street in 2008 with the demise of Bear Stearns and Lehman Brothers, was a classic bank run. Only this time the runs were on investment banks by professional money managers.

Bank Death Spirals

As more and more subprime mortgages defaulted, the effects rippled through the financial system. But the panic seemed overwrought and puzzling. The overall size of the subprime market was only $1 trillion dollars out of a total mortgage market of $11 trillion dollars, and only a fraction of these defaulted. The grand total loss on these mortgages was an insubstantial amount compared to the wreckage suffered by the rest of the economy and the size of the banks that were brought down. What is even more puzzling is that some of the banks, such as Northern Rock, had only a tiny exposure to subprime. So what was going on?

The answer, from Brunnermeier and others like Lasse Pedersen of NYU who study bank runs, is the financial crisis was largely a *liquidity* squeeze. Banks held long-term assets but needed liquidity— that is, immediate cash—in the short term. The afflicted banks, in many cases, didn't necessarily have fundamental problems in terms of their overall businesses, at least not initially. Nor were individual creditors irrationally panicking or driven by emotion, although it certainly seemed that way. Instead, liquidity dried up and banks were caught short.

Brunnermeier and Pedersen have developed a theory that helps explain this; they use the term "liquidity spiral" to describe the near-death (or death) spiral of banks. Think of it as a vicious circle, made up of several components. With credit contracting everywhere, banks were desperately trying to sell mortgage-backed securities, but they found no one was bidding on them; everyone was in a similar situation of a weakening balance sheet. As banks laid off employees, a phone call to another banker to see if they were interested in buying a CDO might have been met with, "That person doesn't work here anymore." Or maybe no one was there to pick up the phone.

The driver was that the amplification mechanism that had created so much easy credit out of securitized mortgages began to work in reverse. As mortgage-backed securities fell in value, the assets of the banks holding them fell in value. The highly leveraged banks, in order not to become even more leveraged, had to tighten their balance sheets. They sold mortgage-backed securities to generate cash and maintain their leverage ratios. The selling in turn drove their prices lower, reducing the value of the assets yet again and reducing credit again (what Pedersen and Brunnermeier call the "loss spiral").

On top of the losses, credit standards tightened, realistically so for once. Asset prices were becoming more volatile and the risk of defaults increased, so banks began to ration their lending. When they increased margin requirements, this hurt other banks and traders, forcing them to sell, further reducing prices and credit (a so-called "margin spiral"). A prudent move by individual banks only made liquidity dry up faster. This rational response to a risky market made the overall market riskier.

These mechanisms reinforced each other. All worked at the same time. Losses led to selling, and selling led to losses.

This spiral afflicting credit markets largely explains what happened at Northern Rock. Although it held few mortgage-backed securities, its creditors—mostly other banks—did, and they called in their loans when they began to deleverage. This caused a crisis at Northern Rock. Its assets were primarily long term, and it was impossible to obtain short-term funding, making it "uniquely vulnerable to the shrinkage of lender balance sheets," according to Hyun Shin, a Princeton economist who has studied Northern Rock. The bank run by individual investors was a response to, not a cause of this problem. The more damaging run was by the institutional creditors who withdrew their assets because of their own problems. As Shin notes, "Although the television images of retail depositors outside branch offices were dramatic, they were not the proximate cause of the liquidity crisis at Northern Rock.... Instead, it was the short-term and medium-term creditors who had previously bought Northern Rock paper but who withdrew from the market." Order was only restored when the Bank of England intervened to provide needed liquidity.

Liquidity spirals swept across the financial system. Markets become gridlocked. Corporate credit froze. Extremely esoteric asset classes such as ARSs (auction rate securities), a form of debt used by municipalities, seized up. ARSs became front-page news, in part because they had been sold to wealthy investors as equivalent to cash, but no one had mentioned the potential liquidity risks. Hedge funds, which relied upon easy credit for their leverage, were caught in their own version of liquidity spirals and were forced to sell assets into illiquid markets. As a result, most hedge funds lost money during the first nine months of 2008. According to *The New York Times*, during that time period only 1 in 50 hedge funds was truly a big winner. Almost everyone else in the financial world was ensnared, one way or another, in the contraction of credit. Even Lou Ranieri, the father of securitization, did not emerge unscathed. He was chairman and cofounder of Franklin Bank, which had loaned heavily to builders in Florida and California and hence lost most of its market value. The bank was seized by the government in November 2008.

Looking back at the wreckage of investment banks and hedge funds, Markus Brunnermeier told me, "From a social-planning perspective, it is not a bad thing that hedge funds take on unavoidable tail risks (the risks of extreme events). It is better that the rich guys who could afford it suffer rather than the poor guys who can't. The bad thing is that many of the systematic risks could have been avoided if anyone had acted against the bubbles earlier."

Later, when the stock market crashed, the situation changed. The crisis was no longer just a problem for hedge funds or investment banks. The whole country, indeed the whole world, suffered. As Brunnermeier acknowledged, "Now we are in a different phase."

37

Euphoria, Fear, and Economics: A Psychological Autopsy of the Crisis

Testifying before Congress about the origins of the 2008 panic, former Fed Chairman Alan Greenspan said:

> "It was the failure to properly price such risky assets that precipitated the crisis.... The whole intellectual edifice collapsed in the summer of last year because the data inputted into the risk management models generally covered only the past two decades, a period of euphoria.

Greenspan added:

> "Those of us who have looked to the self-interest of lending institutions to protect shareholder's equity (myself especially) are in a state of shocked disbelief...."

Those of us who believe that humans, including humans building advanced computer models, are prone to intuitive mistakes such as overconfidence, myopia, and naive extrapolation, are not in a state of shocked disbelief. In fact, it is shocking that Greenspan was shocked. One core finding of behavioral economics is that rational self-interest does not automatically protect people from hurting their own financial interests, particularly when left to their own devices.

These same cognitive limitations and intuitive failures may explain why so few economists were able to correctly forecast the crash. Even in hindsight, it is complicated and hard to explain what happened—and it was that much harder in foresight. Important, securitization bridged many sectors and industries, from real-estate to credit markets. It was almost too wide for our narrowly framed mental perspectives to fully take in. People who saw there was a real-estate bubble were unlikely to have known about the inadequacies of the ratings agencies, the leverage used by the banks, and the fragility of the securitization system. Similarly, experts in securitization were so immersed in their subfield that they missed the bigger picture. Most financial pundits focus on the stock market but know little about credit markets, and so were caught flat-footed by disruptions in this area. To anticipate exactly how problems in U.S. subprime mortgages would translate into a freeze in credit markets such as auction rate securities or bank runs in Europe was too expansive for any one human brain to handle.

Within securitization itself, the opaqueness of products made any sort of clear assessment challenging. Even Lou Ranieri told *The Wall Street Journal* that the constant changes and complexity of the industry were becoming "almost overwhelming."

Last, but not least, until it finally crashed, the industry was still making money, lots of money. This was proof enough that everything was in order for most investors, bankers, journalists, economists, and anyone else who cared to ask.

♦ ♦ ♦

The overall crisis involved many players with many motives, who operated on many layers. It was partially behavioral in character, based on faulty intuition and irrational beliefs, and partially the result of a poorly designed financial system that actually encouraged excessive risk-taking. In some layers, gut mistakes and naive intuitive errors dominated. In others, such as the deleveraging and the resulting liquidity spirals, coldly rational decisions could still be consistent with ruinous outcomes for the market on the whole.

Behavioral errors certainly dominated the heart of the crisis, the real-estate bubble. Homeowners speculating in South Florida were overly optimistic about the future price of their homes and their ability to repay mortgages they could never really afford. The collective belief was real-estate prices could only go up. However, mortgages brokers involved in these shady deals in sunny places were not operating on such false beliefs. They were acting rationally, although not necessarily ethically, as they pushed through deals without bearing any of the risks.

The investment banks present more of a mixed bag. You can tell both a "behavioral story" and a "rational behavior/bad incentives" story to describe the banks' actions, and it's hard to distinguish which one was the primary driver. Probably both were involved. For many involved, misaligned incentives and simple greed may have the most explanatory power. Bankers' pay was not necessarily linked to long-term performance. Unless there were "clawbacks" in place forcing them to someday return their bonuses, it wasn't really their problem if things fell apart after they left. But the CEOs running the banks were themselves the largest shareholders. Misaligned incentives don't fully explain their actions. Psychology, particularly overconfidence, provides greater insights here than traditional economics.

Behavioral insights are also useful for understanding the problems in the computer models used by the banks. However sophisticated the models may have looked, the assumptions their programmers used were stunningly naive. As Greenspan noted, the models understated the true risks involved and were clearly too optimistic—on the way up as well as on the way down. On the way up, the models failed to factor in the possibility of a national real-estate downturn. On the way down, the models viewed each bank's deleveraging decisions in isolation. They failed to factor in the spillover effect onto other banks and the liquidity spirals that might result. They failed to consider the risk that the bank itself might be vulnerable to liquidity spirals from other banks as they deleveraged. They failed to recognize that every bank was deploying similar models and was likely to react the same way, creating a financial contagion. Each bank only thought about itself and modeled its own actions. This lack of empathy isn't surprising coming from an investment bank, but it turned out to be crucially blinkered and ultimately self-destructive. It meant the banks didn't anticipate that everyone would try to sell off their mortgage-backed securities at once and there would be no buyers.

But not everyone buys into the idea that the errors in the banks' models was merely a case of naiveté driven by basic intuitive errors. The bankers themselves, at the sub-CEO level, may have known exactly what they were conveniently forgetting to include in the models. What looks like impulsive decisions or recklessness may have been rational actions that served their own self-interests: to make the most money.

This is exactly the view of Dirk Jenter of Stanford Business School who studies corporate incentives. Here is his perspective:

> "My personal take is that a lot of guys in the investment banks must have known what they were doing was screwy. They were running bets that were going to pay off every year until they went wrong, and when they went wrong they wiped everyone out completely. But every year you are taking out 2% of assets under management and 20% of profits, so you could easily be taking home $5 million a year. When things go bust, you stick everyone else with the losses and say 'I'm so sorry.'"

Jenter makes an analogy to selling California earthquake insurance. This could be a fantastic business. California could go through many seismically quiet years, with the agent taking home a nice premium year after year. When the big one occurs, as it inevitably does, the insurer declares bankruptcy. What prevents this scam is that the California insurance market is tightly regulated. But the credit default swap industry isn't.

The analogy almost precisely describes the actions of AIG's London unit, which wrote insurance on CDOs using credit default swaps. Every investor needed this insurance against a CDO defaulting, and AIG's London operation, consisting of only 377 employees in a corporation with over 116,000, was there to help. It wrote contract after contract, generating profits of half a billion dollars a year, with the average employee paid $1 million a year. But when the big one came, AIG had trouble honoring the insurance contracts. The losses for the London unit were $25 billion in three months alone. The top employees left and retreated to their London townhouses, with most of their fortunes intact.

As Jenter says, "The profits weren't big enough to make it worthwhile for the company, but they were big enough for the board to pay attention." This is an indication of deeply flawed incentives favoring the individual over the company, and also possibly a dysfunctional organization. So why didn't the CEO or the board rein in this sort of operation?

Here many CEOs claim they had no choice. They had to take on the extra risks and keep making money or lose their jobs. In a competitive market environment, they would have been punished if their return on equity was lower than their peers. In another words, the market made them do it. They were just following orders (from shareholders). However you look at it, they argue they are blameless. They were riding the subprime tiger and it was just too dangerous to get off. Therefore, the CEOs made the rational choice, just not, it turns out, the right one for their shareholders, their company, and even their own long-term interests.

Charles Prince, then CEO of Citibank, put forward this argument quite succinctly. In July 2007 he offered a comment that would turn out to be both notorious and prescient in light of what followed. Said Prince, "When the music stops, in terms of liquidity, things will be complicated. But as long as the music is playing, you've got to get up and dance. We're still dancing."

The colossal flaw in the flawed incentives argument is that the CEOs set many of the incentives themselves, for their employees, but even for the overall market. The CEOs of the big New York investment banks had a huge amount of political leverage in Washington. If they were worried about their competitors' actions and the prudent need to collectively curtail risks, they didn't show it. Rather than

ramping down risk, they ramped it up. They did this in concert, collectively. Together, in 2004, they successfully lobbied the SEC to
increase the amount of financial leverage their banks were allowed
use. In a simple and superficial meeting on April 28, 2004, that lasted
less than an hour, with a lot of self-congratulatory chuckles, the SEC
relaxed the rules on leverage. The banks could double their bets on
mortgage-backed securities without adding to their reserves. (You can
listen to an audio recording of this meeting that was to lead to the
demise of the Western banking system, on the SEC's website:
http://www.sec.gov/cgi-bin/goodbye.cgi?www.connectlive.com/events/
secopenmeetings/sec-042804-archive.asx [second hour]).

Only five investment banks were initially granted this special
right to relax their net capital adequacy requirements and increase
the leverage they could use: Lehman, Bear Stearns, Merrill Lynch,
Morgan Stanley, and Goldman Sachs. Within five years, none was to
survive as investment banks. The first three failed or had to be sold
off. The CEO of the last bank on this list later resurfaced as Treasury
Secretary overseeing the bailout: Henry M. Paulson, Jr. Rather than
being victims of the system, the CEOs were the system.

♦ ♦ ♦

Looking over the wreckage of the U.S. financial system, and the
flawed decisions that led to the crash, Alan Greenspan took up the
behaviorist banner. Traditional economics and economic motives
couldn't explain everything that went wrong. Instead, he laid the ultimate blame on the psychology of investors and in particular on the
irrationality of super-rational banking forecasting models in not fac-
toring in human behavior. Greenspan's new found enthusiasm for the
behaviorist approach sounds surprising, even contradictory, in terms
of his belief in the rational self-interest of investors, but Greenspan
himself embodies the complexity of human motives and experience.
He has a background in jazz and toured nationally in a jazz band. (I
don't know if he ever played with jazz saxophonist Paul Desmond,

who forecast that bankers would cause the end of the world.) And Greenspan's policies at the Fed always had a certain improv quality.

The former chairman of the U.S. Federal Reserve told Congress:

"The current financial crisis in the U.S. is likely to be judged in retrospect as the most wrenching since the end of the Second World War.... The essential problem is that our models—both risk models and econometric models—as complex as they have become, are still too simple to capture the full array of governing variables that drive global economic reality.

"These models do not fully capture what I believe has been, to date, only a peripheral addendum to business-cycle and financial modeling—the innate human responses that result in swings between euphoria and fear that repeat themselves generation after generation with little evidence of a learning curve. Asset-price bubbles build and burst today as they have since the early eighteenth century, when modern competitive markets evolved. To be sure, we tend to label such behavioral responses as nonrational. But forecasters' concerns should be not whether human response is rational or irrational, only that it is observable and systematic.

"This, to me, is the large, missing 'explanatory variable' in both risk-management and macroeconometric models."

Regulation

As Greenspan acknowledged, banks were unable to manage their own risks. Self-regulation failed, and as a result, so did financial markets. One solution to the various failures that Greenspan listed is external regulation from the government, in terms of new laws and regulatory agencies. But finding the right regulatory approach is tough: If people are greedy but rational, that implies a certain regulatory philosophy. If people are greedy but also myopic, overconfident, and prone to fall into a stupor because they are literally drunk on money, that implies something else.

I spoke to Joseph Stiglitz about this. Stiglitz had won a Nobel Prize in economics for his work on information and markets. As an economist, he bridged the academic/policy divide, with numerous political appointments, including chairman of the Council of Economic Advisors for President Clinton and chief economist for the World Bank. His ideas about regulation neatly classified the muddled policy solutions that were floating around during the crisis. I reached Stiglitz by phone when he was on the shuttle about to take off for DC.

"The theory of regulation is based on three different hypotheses, about markets and participants," Stiglitz explained. "The first is that government only needs to demand transparency for competitive markets to work well." According to this hypothesis, if buyers really understood the ingredients in a CDO and the risks, the market would have priced them correctly. Buyers would have shunned the more toxic ones, or at least hesitated before adding them to their portfolio. To use McDonald's as an analogy, if you knew the calories in a Double Quarter Pounder with cheese (740), you might think twice about gobbling one down.

"The second hypothesis is, even if we have transparency and competition, we still need additional regulation to deal with externalities," said Stiglitz. The classic externality is pollution. People downwind from a factory suffer the effects of pollution, but the factory itself pays nothing. Chinese banks damaged by toxic Wall Street assets could reasonably consider these to be a sort of pollution. And Northern Rock, for example, was caught in an externality, a liquidity squeeze created by other banks when they de-leveraged. According to the externality hypothesis, sometimes the government needs to step in to regulate competitive markets to make sure people aren't unfairly impacted by other people's actions.

"The third hypothesis is, people are irrational. And the government has to protect people against their own irrationality," said Stiglitz. "What was going on in these markets reflects irrational behavior in a fundamental sense. Many of the borrowers were not fully educated and were preyed upon. Mortgage guys understood their behavior and maximized their profits at the expense of poor homeowners through things such as teaser rates. This creates capital market imperfections that result from the exploitation."

Markets failed for all three of these reasons. Structured products were opaque and hard to value. In terms of externalities, banks had no incentives to worry about the liquidity spirals and financial contagions they caused when they deleveraged. And, finally, mortgage borrowers, but also bank CEOs, were irrationally exuberant during the boom, and took what turned out to be self-destructive risks.

Although there were regulatory lapses in all these areas, most of the policy discussions only focused on hypothesis number one: the lack of transparency in the system as the cause of the crash. The irrationality of participants got short shrift. "The presumption is greater transparency will solve the problem," said Stiglitz, "but it fails to address underlying issues." If markets are efficient and participants rational, why didn't they demand greater transparency themselves? Why didn't the market provide it, or why weren't the incentives already in place to demand it? This seeming contradiction proves markets and participants aren't fully rational. Or as Stiglitz says of the transparency hypothesis, "It is intellectually inconsistent. They don't have a coherent theory."

In terms of externalities (impacts on parties not directly involved in an economic decision), regulators will have to find ways to prevent banks getting caught in a liquidity squeeze caused by other banks' problems. A better designed financial system could mitigate financial contagions. For a start, rather than just focusing on limits to leverage or the adequacy of the bank's capital reserves, regulators need to consider the liquidity of these reserves so that a bank can withstand a liquidity squeeze.

But what about the *people* involved? What is the response required for his third hypothesis? Here is Stiglitz's suggestion:

> "If participants are irrational, here is what you do. We need to outlaw the behavior of those who are smart who exploit the irrationality of those who are less smart. But even sophisticated people have made the same mistakes repeatedly, of underestimating price declines or what they think of as 'low' probability events."

Stiglitz had many ideas of how to restructure regulation: All had the goal of creating a newly reformed financial system that is less fragile and more stable than today's. He argues for the creation of a "Financial Products Safety Commission" that evaluates the safety and appropriateness of new financial products. It could create standards for products and also reveal their risks.

In addition to increasing the transparency of financial instruments, it would be useful to make the motives of the people in the system more transparent. This includes letting the public know the fees mortgage lenders, ratings agencies, and bankers get for each deal. But greater transparency also includes confronting individuals with their own irrationality. Borrowers were taking risks they may have preferred to overlook. Says Stiglitz, "You can inform people about the nature of irrationality. You can help them deal with the worst consequences like predatory lending and excessive risk taking."

The truly comprehensive solution, according to Stiglitz, is a regulatory framework that ensures the stability of the system under more robust conditions than participants think of as useful. "We need limits on leverage," he said, "and speed bumps on growth." The analogy to fire codes made at the beginning of this book is appropriate here. People don't like to pay for fire exits when constructing a building.

They tend to underestimate the risk of fire and don't want to pay for the extra protection. Building codes *force* the exits to be part of the building design. Similarly, participants in the financial system underestimated the risk of a financial meltdown, either because distorted incentives meant it was somebody else's problem, or because bankers were in a money-induced stupor. Regulation to prevent future financial catastrophes will have to require banks to build some sort of firewall against these systemic contagions. It will reduce their profits but make life much safer for everyone else.

Regulating markets to protect them from participants' worst instincts could build a stronger U.S. financial system, one capable of dealing with a similar crisis in the future, with limits on the potential damage investors could do to themselves. Yet regulators themselves are, of course, subject to the same biases and irrational impulses as everyone else. Look at the way the U.S. government initially reacted to the crisis. Treasury Secretary Paulson lurched from one rescue attempt to the next. He didn't seem to consistently follow any particular regulatory strategy. One favorite tactic was to try to inspire confidence in the economy through up-beat speeches, but Paulson had no luck with this approach either. Stiglitz says of these efforts: "He may have had experience that rationally he could convince irrational people using irrational arguments, but it didn't work this time."

Paulson's inconsistent responses may best be explained by his background—as an investment banker. The field of behavioral economics studying CEOs shows executives are marked by their experience and background. They rarely change their strategic "style" regardless of the problems confronting them. Paulson brought an investment banker's perspective to his new job, evaluating everything on a case-by-case basis. Bail out Lehman? No. Bail out AIG? Yes. Instead of approaching the problem as a systemic macroeconomic crisis, he viewed each flare up as just another deal.

◆ ◆ ◆

These ideas about different types of government regulation are ways to strengthen the financial system. But what about the individual investor? What sort of self-regulation can improve investment performance? In the concluding part of this book, I look at ways individuals can "debias" their intuitive errors in thinking.

Part VI
Conclusion: Debiasing

38

How Not to Blink in the Face of Financial Panic

We know we make intuitive mistakes when making financial decisions. The real question is, "What to do about it?" This is a much less researched question than identifying the behavioral biases themselves, and it is not an easy one to answer. Very little is known and the challenges are immense: Our cognitive propensities and gut instincts are deeply entrenched from long, long ago. They may have evolved before language, or even before there were people. Animals also rely on rules of thumb to find food and avoid being eaten. But animals don't issue credit ratings or securitize mortgages.

How, then, can we protect ourselves from ourselves? Government regulations are things society can do, but what can individual investors do themselves to debias their own intuitive failures? In terms of financial decisions, the counterintuitive investment strategies discussed throughout the book can lead to better investment performance. But another way to go is through behavioral "interventions," some of them psychological, some of them *physical.* I explore behavioral interventions in the following sections.

Teach Yourself the Science of Finance

"I don't think debiasing is hard to do; I think it is a piece of cake," psychologist Richard Nisbett of the University of Michigan told me. Nisbett's research is about how lay people reason and make inferences about the world. His argument is that society itself, and the spread of scientific knowledge, has been successfully debiasing our decision making since the seventeenth century.

Nisbett claims that in the seventeenth century, the cost of a lifetime annuity for a two-year-old and a 70-year-old were the same. Of course, two year olds didn't have the same life expectancy as today, but the real reason for this error is no one knew how to calculate probabilities. As probability theory and statistics developed, its concepts spread to the population on the whole. People understood the ideas, and no longer had to rely on their intuition and gut instincts to make a statistical decision.

Rather than patiently waiting for new ideas about economics to slowly diffuse in your direction, you can speed up the knowledge transfer by teaching yourself the science of finance. Investors can come to understand that stock markets are random, or almost so, and are very hard to predict outside of a handful of anomalies. Or that widespread investor opinion about the future direction of the market is in fact a contrarian indicator, and is wrong more often than right. The knowledge of the importance of asset allocation to investing is now well known, but the importance of asset *location* is still comparatively obscure. Asset "location" is where you place your assets, such as in a taxable account or a tax-free account such as an IRA or a 401(k). It is a way to minimize your tax bill and grow your returns. The general principal is that you should "locate" your tax-inefficient investments, such as your bonds, in your tax-deferred accounts, where you don't pay immediate taxes on them. In contrast, investments that don't generate heavy tax bills, such as index funds, belong in your taxable accounts.

Knowing the science of investing includes recognizing its limitations. One is that economics is a social science, despite its grandiose claims to be as rigorous and precise as physics. Although behavioral finance has dramatically improved the empirical relevance of economics, it is itself still a very young social science with many unknowns.

The recent financial crisis also showed that most economic "forecasting" is largely backward-looking, using historical data and statistical relationships for inputs. In psychological terms, it is too narrowly "framed." When market processes changed during the crisis, these historical numbers offered no guidance. Correlations all converged to one and everything went down together. The financial crisis should have caused a crisis in confidence in economic forecasting, but this doesn't appear to be the case.

Financial economics is also too U.S.-centric. Other countries have had very different stock market histories from that of the U.S. and an international perspective gives a very different picture of the risks involved in investing in equities. Researchers Elroy Dimson, Paul Marsh, and Mike Staunton, who study international equity returns, found: "For the majority of countries, stocks did not provide a consistently positive real return over the long run, defined as an interval of 20 years." Historically, investors needed to hold equities for 20 to 30 years to be assured of positive returns in Swedish, British, Swiss, Irish, and Dutch markets. It is even worse in other countries. According to Dimson, "Japanese, French, German, and Spanish investors would have needed greater patience to be sure of a positive real return; they would have required an investment horizon of 50–60 years. Italian and Belgian investors would have needed an investment horizon of more than 70 years." The conventional wisdom that stocks are safe in the long run needs to be seriously questioned or at least refined to ask if this is still true of U.S. stocks, or will equity returns come to resemble those of Italy and Belgium? And how long is the long run? Waiting 70 years for stocks to do well is too long.

Use a Financial Advisor...for Psychological Reasons

Investors turn to financial advisors for their expertise or because they don't have the time or interest to manage their portfolios themselves. But the greatest value in using a financial advisor might be psychological: They act as a line of defense against our own worst intuitive impulses. They take the emotion out of investing.

"Financial advisors are a great assistance mechanism," the behavioral economist Meir Statman told me. "When people are terrified, they do what is natural to them, which usually makes for bad investing. The advisor can help you think about it, slowing you down for awhile in the hope that a cooling-off period will help."

The financial planning industry is itself recognizing the value of this psychological function. Advisors are emphasizing their financial coaching skills. Just the way athletes turn to a coach for discipline, instruction, and encouragement, many investors find turning to a financial advisor is the easiest way to reach their retirement savings goals.

Although financial advisors can help us overcome our natural biases, we have to be aware of their biases. The obvious one is money: It's a business and they are there to maximize their fees. Using a fee-only advisor with no hidden commissions helps. The advisor may promise "open architecture," meaning he or she can select investments from anywhere, not just his or her broker/ dealer. But the advisor may be pressured by the broker/dealer to push its own products anyway. As a client, push back if you see too many funds from the advisor's parent company appearing in your portfolio.

The subtler and more significant problem with advisors has to do with taxes. Taxes are a bigger drag on returns than commissions or investment fees, yet they don't get the same degree of attention from advisors or clients. Financial advice is usually done on a pretax basis. Advisors, almost without exception, report returns pretax, comparing them to a benchmark before any taxes are taken out. This is a systemic problem of the industry and an area where clients are poorly served. You may look like you are beating the S&P—until you consider what you investment looks like after taxes and fees, too.

Take the personal investment performance of Rob Arnott, founder of Research Associates. In his personal investments in the early 1990s, his pretax returns were something approaching 18%

annually. The market was only returning 12%. He thought he was doing spectacularly well—until he considered the tax hit. His after-tax returns were only something like 15%, still slightly better than the market, but much worse than he had expected. Chastened by this reality, Arnott decided to make taxes a front-burner issue in his investing, and he helped develop tax-efficient index funds. He also was galvanized to write (with Tad Jeffrey) the breakthrough article, "Is Your Alpha Big Enough to Cover Its Taxes?" This study asked if an investment manager's market-beating return, or alpha, would be large enough to offset the tax bill that came from active management. For many investment strategies, the answer is clearly no, and a passive index would provide better after-tax returns.

Clients, working with their advisors, need to make tax efficiency an integral part of the financial-planning process. For instance, after the 2008 plunge in the stock market, the natural temptation of many investors was to hunker down and not sell anything, hoping the market would recover. Had they instead been engaged in tax-loss harvesting, painful as it might have been, they could have enjoyed years of no capital gains taxes.

The systematic solution is to have advisors report performance on an after-tax basis and create portfolios with this objective in mind. But until clients start demanding this type of reporting, advisors have little incentive to provide it. The failure, therefore, rests largely on the shoulders of the clients. The underlying challenge is the biased way we think: Taxes are hidden until after the fact, when we have to pay them. In contrast, expenses and commissions are explicitly reported and therefore get our attention. And because taxes aren't salient, investors don't fully take them into account, and make poor investment choices from an after-tax perspective. So the next time a financial advisor excitedly tells you about different possible investment "opportunities," be sure to ask about the likely *after* tax returns before you decide.

Remind your advisor, and yourself, of one basic truth of investing: It's not how much you make; it's how much you get to keep.

Form a Group

Some of the richest families in America are members of private discussion groups where they share wealth-management ideas and other information. There are many such groups, most of them hidden from public view. Typically, they do not allow brokers or consultants as members (although they can guest lecture). Instead, it is a peer-to-peer movement, of rich families for rich families. These families have special needs, many of them psychological. Their guilt about their good fortune is one; the best way to meet their philanthropic objectives is another. Additionally, these sorts of families are tempting targets for conmen such as Bernie Madoff and his Ponzi scheme.

Other families have needs, too, and a group setting can be useful for addressing financial and psychological issues common to everyone, not just the super rich. Hersh Shefrin, one of the founders of behavioral finance, is quite specific about what form such an investment group should take: "I think it should be modeled on a 12-step program. You can apply some of the 12-step principles, recognizing there is a problem, supporting each other, with a great deal of honesty and mutual trust." He adds, "Investors hate to feel stupid. It's hard to admit what you don't know or mistakes you have made unless everybody else is in the same boat."

A financial discussion group can put in place debiasing mechanisms not available to the individual investor. On our own we tend to follow the path of least resistance. It is easier to overcome our self-control problems with the support of a group. Weight Watchers is an example. In a group framework, everyone can advance together to reach a common goal.

For the group to work, someone involved needs to understand the theoretical concepts in finance (including behavioral finance), so the group doesn't end up sharing worst practices as opposed to best. The Beardstown Ladies Investment club is an example of what can go wrong. This was a financial group made up mostly of grandmothers that was famous in the 1990s for its ability to beat the market. After several best-selling investment advice books, it was revealed the ladies had made a calculation error and their club was in fact underperforming the market.

Drink the Kool-Aid

We can make decisions either analytically or intuitively using the two decision systems we have at our disposal. Relying on the instant "blink" system is easy; thinking analytically and actively suppressing our intuition is slower and harder. A newer area of psychological research shows there is a physical component to these two systems. This research has identified ways that make it easier for us to turn to our analytical system when it is called for.

E.J. Masicampo, a psychology graduate student at Florida State working with psychologist Roy Baumeister, has devised a brilliant and complex experiment that shows these two systems at work. The experiment shows how the body reacts with the mind, and how certain physical states are associated with certain mental states. It all comes down to sugar.

"Analytical decisions are hard; intuitive decisions are relatively easy. When your glucose is depleted from a mentally strenuous task, you start making choices in a less effortful way; you go with the easy," Masicampo explained. His experiment demonstrated, he says, that "those without the sugar stopped effortful thinking. It felt better to them to go with their intuition. But this led to less rational decisions."

Here is the experiment: Participants are told to watch a split-screen video. On the top half of the screen, a woman is talking, but the video is on mute. On the bottom half of the screen, words are flashed: "street," "shoe," "lamp," "green." The words have no common theme and have been chosen to be as neutral as possible. The experimental subjects are told to focus only on the woman's expression, to ignore the words and to interpret nonverbal clues to her emotions. They have to work very hard to figure out what she is trying to communicate. The viewers believe they are in a psychological experiment to understand nonverbal behavior. It is true they are participating in a psychological experiment, but instead it is one about mental fatigue and decision making. Showing participants the woman and the words together is designed merely to tax their brain. This depletes glucose, a well-established physiological fact.

Then they are offered a cool glass of lemonade. Some people get lemonade made with real sugar; others get it sweetened with Splenda. Although this doesn't seem important to the participants, it is crucial to what comes next.

Now the subjects of this experiment are asked to make a tough decision, in this case choosing among apartments. One apartment is really close to campus but is kind of small. The second is far away but is huge. And some students are shown a third choice—an apartment that is even farther off campus, but is quite small. The third choice is to throw them off. Psychologically, it is known as a "decoy." It is in every respect worse than the other two.

It turns out that those who drank the lemonade with sugar made more rational decisions than those who drank the lemonade sweetened with Splenda. They were less swayed by the decoy. Those who only had the Splenda made the more intuitive decision—they paid a great deal of attention to the decoy although it shouldn't have been considered at all because it was an irrelevant choice. In short, participants with depleted glucose were irrationally swayed by the decoy and might even choose it, whereas nondepleted participants ignored it.

Says Masicampo: "The experiment demonstrates that glucose is a resource that is depleted during tough mental decisions. Glucose needs to be at an optimal level for self-control and decision making to operate."

When people are mentally exhausted and their glucose is depleted, they are more likely to go with the intuitive choice, and not to think as clearly. Ingestion of sugar reduces our reliance on intuitive decision making. We have the energy to think more analytically. So when facing an important decision, one that requires concentration, make sure your glucose level is replenished and stable. (Masicampo tells me that an elevated glucose level doesn't give you any edge.) Sleeping on a decision is one way to accomplish this; it will restore your depleted glucose. So does having sugar. So go ahead, drink the Kool-Aid, provided it is sweetened.

Oh, Behave! Better Behavior Courtesy of Behavioral Economics

Instead of relying on top-down regulation, or leaving everything in the hands of the individual, an intermediate approach to debiasing comes from behavioral economics itself. It is appealing to those who are skeptical of heavy-handed government regulation and believe people can ultimately make good decisions but need a little help getting there. The idea is to "nudge" people in the right direction, but not insist upon it. The beauty of these "nudges" is they use our own biases, which behaviorally economics has so carefully identified, such as inertia and myopia, to help us, not hurt us. If you are enrolled in a 401(k), you may have been exposed to behavioral economics nudges without realizing it.

The area of greatest activity has been finding ways to overcome people's resistance to saving more for retirement. If you have access to a 401(k), consider yourself lucky. Only about half the American workforce is now covered by any sort of employer-provided retirement plan. Yet those who are eligible for a 401(k) do not make full use

of it. On average, they take about two years to enroll with many not
bothering to enroll at all.

Economists David Laibson, Brigitte Madrian, and James Choi
were conducting a study analyzing 401(k) participation rates of
employees eligible to join 401(k)s when they noticed something
strange. One employer had a sky-high percentage of its workforce
enrolled in its 401(k) plan, much higher than its competitors. This
wasn't the result of a conscious strategy; it was an accident of history.
It had to do with the way its 401(k) plan was designed. Employees
were automatically enrolled in the 401(k) when they were hired, but
had the option to opt out if they wanted. For virtually every other
employer, it is the other way around: If employees wanted to enroll,
they had to actively make the choice to join and sign up themselves.

Laibson and his team immediately saw the importance of this tiny
change in 401(k) plan design. It all came down to what is known in
behavioral economics and benefits consulting as "defaults." The default
position was enrollment in the plan. Not enrolling required effort and
activity by employees, whereas if they did nothing, they were automatically signed up. Simply by setting the default position to enrollment,
the economists could dramatically increase participation in 401(k)s.

The reason is behavioral: Inertia rules our 401(k) decisions. The
default position guides our choice much more than thinking rationally about the decision would suggest. Of course, employees who for
some reason didn't want to save for retirement still have an out, and
nothing is mandatory. But opting out of the 401(k) would mean overcoming inertia, and actually ticking a box to say they didn't want to
enroll.

Behavioral economists have also found ways to get us to con-
tribute a higher percentage of our salaries to our 401(k). The
intervention is known as "Save More Tomorrow." It was devised by
behavioral economists Shlomo Benartzi and Richard Thaler (who is
co-author of *Nudge*). Employees precommit to automatically

increase the percentage of their paycheck that goes to their 401(k) each time they get a raise, when they are least likely to notice the difference. What makes it even easier, from a behavioral perspective, is this also means most of the increases are in the future, so it is not so painful at the time of the decision. Thaler and Benartzi have been able to raise the average 401(k) contributions of an employee from less than 4% of their salary to over 11% of their salary.

Defaults and similar benefit plan design ideas are ricocheting throughout the policy world. There is talk of implementations of defaults when it comes to retirement income choices, health insurance, or really anywhere people have to make a decision. Defaults are a behavioral economics success story. Academics have found a way to translate theory into practice to improve people's lives.

Have they been oversold? It depends where and how they are used. Defaults inarguably work in areas where people don't have strong preference or much knowledge, such as 401(k)s. But it is ridiculous to think they would work for institutional investors such as hedge funds. The credit crisis involved decisions by insiders with very strong preferences and a lot of knowledge. Senior bankers were busy crafting ways to use complex derivatives to get around existing regulation. I doubt a friendly nudge would have the same influence on a bank as a push and shove in the form of laws requiring more liquid reserves.

A final question hangs over 401(k) defaults, the billion- or trillion-dollar question: "How much do they really increase savings?" They increase 401(k) participation and contributions, but participants might offset this by reducing savings elsewhere. They might put less money aside for their savings account or investment account. Or they might just borrow more against their 401(k). Currently no one knows if the 401(k) interventions are crowding out other saving. Although defaults look immensely promising as a way to improve our savings behavior, not all their side effects are currently known.

39

A Summing Up: Twilight of the Gods

Writing about the end of the Soviet Union in his book *Imperium*, the Polish writer Ryszard Kapuscinski observed:

> "Just before the breakup of the USSR, the view of that country as a model of the most stable and durable system in the world had gained wide acceptance among Western Sovietologists. There was not one American political scientist who predicted the collapse of the USSR."

Kapuscinski argued that the process of disintegration had in fact been underway for years, but Western political scientists had "difficulties understanding what this was all about." He has an additional comment:

> "Almost no prognoses about the contemporary world come true. Futurology is in crisis. It has lost its prestige. The human imagination, shaped for thousands of years by a small, simple, and static world, today cannot grasp, is no match for, the reality that surrounds it."

The near collapse of the U.S. and Western financial system did not mark an end to Western capitalism, but it was a close call and a shock to a system everyone assumed was secure and even infallible. Western analysts and economists also had difficulties understanding what it was all about. They took investment banks' inexplicably large profits as proof of the banks' superior wisdom, rather than an indication of extreme risk-taking. They didn't see the growing fragility. The danger turned out not to be from some unpredictable external event, a "black swan" as they are sometimes called, but instead came from within, inherent in the system itself and the way it was designed.

Commentators instead had proclaimed a "brave new world" in finance. A 2006 IMF report titled, "Global Financial System Resilience in the Face of Cyclical Challenge," is typical. It noted, "A wider dispersion of credit risk has 'de-risked' the banking sector. It is widely acknowledged, meanwhile, that holding of credit risk by a diverse multitude of investors increases the ability of the financial system as a whole to absorb potential shocks." As almost everyone agreed, the modern financial system was unparalleled in history in its flexibility, profitability, efficiency, and ultimately resiliency.

The failures of these analysts to see that the financial system was in fact becoming more and more in danger of collapse is comparable to the intellectual bankruptcy of Western Sovietology. Nonetheless, these same experts remain employed today (mostly) on Wall Street or in academia. Few seem contrite. Instead they are busy, very busy, working on research reports, appearing on TV and radio, still confidently offering their prognostications about the stock market, real estate, or where to invest now. They are still willing to share their view of the future. The more interesting question is, "Why are we still listening?"

The dysfunctional structure of the securitization *system* had been evident for years. Mortgage borrowers were allowed to take out mortgages with no hope of repaying them. Mortgage lenders could still profit while passing on the problem to someone else. The agencies rating the CDOs (collateralized debt obligations) were paid by the issuers, not the buyers. Credit default swaps were not traded on open exchanges, which increased the risks for everyone involved. Banks had perversely designed incentives. Bankers were paid to take extreme risks and did not personally suffer the consequences if they miscalculated. In the larger financial system, banks maintained capital reserves as required, but these were not liquid reserves and offered no protection against a liquidity spiral. Nor did banks have to worry about the spillover effects onto other banks' balance sheets when they had to quickly sell assets. Regulators allowed, even encouraged all this to happen and refused to lean against the wind of the growing bubbles. The system, though vast, was jerry-built and immature, resembling something thrown together in an emerging economy, not an advanced one. It had an inadequate infrastructure—the rules, regulations, and institutions that could have provided stability in a downturn. America's crumbling roads and bridges are one infrastructural problem, but the country's financial infrastructure is comparably deficient or worse.

Why didn't anyone see this ahead of time? The problem is partially ideological. Everyone thought free markets could solve these problems by themselves and self-correct the institutional and regulatory failings, such as poor incentives, lack of transparency, vulnerability to systemic risks, and unchecked irrational behavior by investors. Instead, new institutions and regulations need to be put in place for competitive free markets to function. Good regulation, rather than stifling competition, can encourage it. And without good regulation markets can fail. During the credit crisis, markets and financial institutions did fail. The ironic result is America may now have to suffer under Soviet-style nationalized industries and banks.

But ultimately the failure to foresee the crisis is psychological. The collapse was beyond belief. The Soviet analogy holds: No one could imagine it. Our impoverished intuition, really our imagination, which evolved to deal with simple questions such as "Does it look like rain?" or "Does she like me?" couldn't handle it. It was outside our narrow and fixed way of thinking.

This is all clear in hindsight. But hindsight is just another psychological bias, and a particularly pernicious one. In hindsight we know we shouldn't have bet on that long-shot horse. Or sold that winning stock. Or invested in that mutual fund that seemed like such a winner at the time, only to watch it stumble after we bought it. Or put so much of our 401(k) into equities, which melted away during the crisis. You mustn't blame yourself for making decisions based on information that seemed correct at the time and only in hindsight was shown to be wrong. You didn't know then what you know now. But now you do know more: about how your intuition and instincts work when it comes to finance, and that you should have second thoughts about your first impressions, particularly when it comes to investing. You can glide through life, trusting your instincts and intuition to make decisions for you. Or armed with conscious deliberation, you can make more thoughtful financial choices. Should you go with your gut or your mind? The decision is yours.

INDEX

Numerics

401(k)
   behavioral economics, 257-259
   portfolios, 55

A

advisors, financial, 251-254
aggregation failure, 210
aggressive CEOs, 183
AIG, credit default swaps, 238
airline travel, shrouded
   prices, 160
aligning incentives, 198
alpha, 48
   persistence, 49
American Home Mortgage, 228
amplification mechanisms, 223
analysts, stock, 67-71
analytical intelligence, 5-8
animal spirits, 106
annuities, 39-45
   framing, 44
   guaranteed death benefits, 44
AOL, 79
Arnott, Rob, 15-16, 252
ARSs (auction rate securities), 232
asks, 208
Asness, Cliff, 87
asset location, 250
auction rate securities (ARSs), 232
Austrian, Bob, 30
availability heuristics, 97

B

Baker, Dean, 227
Baker, Malcolm, 28
Balloon Analogue Risk Task
   (BART), 65
bank death spirals, 230-233
bank models, 241
   errors in, 237
Bank of America, 203
bank runs, 229-233
   liquidity spiral, 231
BART (Balloon Analogue Risk
   Task), 65
basketball, hot streaks, 116-118
Baumeister, Roy, 255
Bear Stearns, 199, 228
Beardstown Ladies Investment
   Club, The, 255
Becker, Boris, 133
behavior
   how our behavior damages
     investments, 51-53
   of CEOs, investing based on,
     197-198
behavioral economics, 21-25
   debiasing, 257-259
   dividends, 27-31
   history of, 105-107
behavioral errors, housing
   crisis, 236
Benartzi, Shlomo, 258
Bernanke, Ben, 156

biases
   coin tosses, 143
   favorite long-shot bias, 109-112
   inertia, 105
   mood and money, 103-105
bids, 208
Blink, 147
BNP Paribas, 228
bond duration, 34
bonds, 33-34
   callable bonds, 37
   choosing, 37
   diversification, 35
   high-yield bonds, 34
   junk bonds, 34
   municipal bonds, 36-37
Boren, Caroline, 30
Brown, Jeffrey, 40-41
Brunnermeier, Markus, 229
bubbles, 207
Buffett, Warren, 73-76, 197
business models, credit cards,
   156-157
buyback anomaly, 78-80

C

callable bonds, 37
car accidents, 177-180
case-based decision making,
   129-130
casinos, 135-136
catering theory, 30
Cayne, James, 199
CDO (collateralized debt
   obligation), 220-225
CDS (credit default swap), 220
CEOs
   aggressive CEOs, 183
   conservative CEOs, 183
   firing, 195-196
   hubris, 189-192
   investing in companies based on
      CEO behavior, 197-198
   strategic styles, 183-186
   superstar CEOs, 192-194
   Wall Street CEOs, 199-203

chart, NFL draft, 126-129
Choi, James, 56, 258
choosing bonds, 37
Cisco, 51
Citibank, 239
clawbacks, 237
coin tosses, 143-144
collateralized debt obligation
   (CDO), 220, 225
commodities, oil, 15
Community Reinvestment Act
   (CRA), 217
Compaq, 190
Connors, John, 30
conscious decision making, 5-8
conservative CEOs, 183
corporate boards, firing CEOs, 196
corporate incentives, 238-239
counterfactuals, 113-116
Couric, Katie, 170
CRA (Community Reinvestment
   Act), 217
credit cards, 155-156
   business models, 156-157
   shrouded prices, 159-162
   snap judgment and interest
      rates, 158-159
credit default swap (CDS), 220
credit risk, 262

D

Darien Gap, 61
De Bondt, Werner, 106
debiasing
   behavioral economics, 257-259
   financial advisors, 251-254
   financial discussion groups,
      forming, 254-255
   glucose levels, 255-257
   learning the science of fiance,
      249-251
December effect, momentum, 86
decision making, 120-122
   case-based decision making,
      129-130
   conscious decision making, 5-8

financial planning, 123-124
glucose levels, 255-257
shared decision making, 169
Desmond, Paul, 240
Diaconis, Persi, 143-144
Dimson, Elroy, 251
disposition effect, 22-25
reference points, 24
diversification
bonds, 35
portfolios, 57
dividends, 27-31
Dodd, David, 73
Dunlap, Al, 186, 194
duration, bonds, 35

E

economics, behavioral, 21-25
debiasing, 257-259
dividends, 27-31
history of, 105-107
effect of money on the brain,
17-18
emotions, mood and money,
103-105
Endostatin, 83
Engel, Kirsten, 167
EntreMed, 83-84
errors
in bank models, 237
in judgment, 19
evolution, gut instincts and, 3-5
exotics, 110

F

Fama, Eugene, 78
Fannie Mae, 217
favorite long-shot bias, 109-112
fear, 214
Fields, Herman C., 155
Figlewski, Stephen, 92
finances, learning science of,
249-251
financial advisors, 251-254

financial bubbles, 207-211
spotting, 211
financial crisis (U.S.), 261-263
financial decisions, 9-10
financial discussion groups,
254-255
financial economics, 251
financial planning, 123-124
risk tolerance, 62
financial planning software, 65
financial services industry,
bubbles, 212
Fiorina, Carly, 190
fire code regulation, 18
firing CEOs, 195-196
First Franklin, 202
first impressions, 3
football
decision making, 120-122
case-based decision making,
129-130
financial planning, 123-124
NFL draft, 125-126
"the chart," 126-129
foreign markets, momentum, 88
frames, 41-42
framing annuities, 44
framing effect, 101
Frank, Richard, 175
Franklin Bank, 232
Frazzini, Andrea, 25, 51-52
Freddie Mac, 217
Frederick, Shane, 100
French, Kenneth, 78
Friedman, Milton, 119
Ft. Lauderdale, 213
Matthew's story, 215-217
Fuld, Richard, 200-203
fuzzy math, 159

G

Gabaix, Xavier, 160
Gallwey, Timothy, 131
gambler's fallacy, 7

gambling, 99-102
  counterfactuals, 113-116
  framing effect, 101
  hot streaks, basketball, 116-118
  long shots, 109-112
  making money, 135-137
    Harrah's, 137-141
GE CEOs, 185
Gestalt approach, 98
Getty Museum, 147
Gill, Sam, 63
Gilovich, Tom, 116
Gladwell, Malcolm, 131, 147
glucose, 256
  debiasing, 255-257
Gould, Stephen Jay, 96
Goyal, Amit, 130
Graham, Benjamin, 21, 73
greed, 214, 236-239
Greene, Graham, 162
Greenspan, Alan, 223-224, 235
Greenwald, Bruce, 74
grocery stores, 140
groups, financial discussion,
  254-255
Grove, Andy, 184
guaranteed death benefits, 44
gut instincts, 2. *See also* intuition
  evolution and, 3-5

H

Hammonds, Dana, 123
Harrah's, 137-141
health insurance, 173-176
  Medicare Part D, 173-175
hedge funds, alpha, 48
herding behavior, 208
heuristics, 8
  availability heuristics, 97
  representative heuristics, 97
high-yield bonds, 34
Hillebrand, Gail, 156
hindsight, 263
history of behavioral economics,
  105-107

HMOs, 75
Holmes, Clayton, 123
Holmes, Susan, 143-144
hot streaks, 116-118
housing crisis, 214-218, 228
  behavioral errors, 236
housing market, Ft. Lauderdale,
  213-214
  Matthew's story, 215-217
Hsee, Christopher, 105
Huberman, Gur, 84
hubris of CEOs, 189-192

I

identifying tolerance for financial
  risk, 64-65
Ikenberry, David, 78
incentives, corporate, 238-239
income, dividend-paying
  stocks, 29
inertia, 105
information aggregation, 210
Inner Game of Tennis, The, 131
inner mental game, 131-134
insurance brokers, 176
Intel, 184
interest rates on credit cards,
  snap judgments, 158-159
intuition, 2-4, 16, 95-98. *See also*
  gut instincts
  long shots, 111
  Prospect Theory, 100-102
  snap judgments, 3
investing
  based on CEO behavior,
    197-198
  risk tolerance and, 62
  value investing, 73-76
    momentum, 87-89
investments, damaging by our
  behavior, 51-53
investors, 112
  dividends, 31
irrational thinking of medical
  patients, 167-171

J

Jacobson, Eric, 36
January effect, momentum, 86
Janus funds, 51
Jensen, Michael, 48
Jensen's alpha, 48
Jenter, Dirk, 195-196, 238
Jones, Andrew, 224-226
junk bonds, 34

K

Kahneman, Daniel, 22, 96
Kaiser, Henry, 75
Kapuscinski, Ryszard, 261
KDB (Korean Development Bank), 202
Kling, Jeffrey, 40
Kolata, Gina, 83
Korean Development Bank (KDB), 202
Kotlikoff, Larry, 65

L

Laibson, David, 160, 258
Lakonishok, Josef, 78
Lamont, Owen, 85
language cues, 4
Lapidus, Alan, 135
Las Vegas, making money by gambling, 135-137
    Harrah's, 137-141
LaSora, Joseph A., 151
Leaf, Ryan, 125
Lehman Brothers, 35, 200-203
Lejuez, Carl, 65
Lerner, Jennifer, 103
"Let it happen," 131
leverage, 217
    SEC, 240
Levin, Jerry, 79
Lewis, Michael, 221
Linda problem, 96-97
liquidity problems, bank runs, 229
liquidity spiral, 231-232

Lo, Andrew, 17-19
Lockheed, 107
long shots, 109-112
long-term care insurance, 44
longevity risk, 44
loss averse, 74
loss spiral, 231
Loveman, Gary, 137
Lynch, Peter, 50

M

Madrian, Brigitte, 258
Magnus, Jan, 132
making money by gambling, 135-137
    Harrah's, 137-141
Malmendier, Ulrike, 190-197
Manning, Archie, 125
Manning, Peyton, 125
margin requirements, 214
margin spiral, 231
Markowitz, Harry, 57-58, 106, 228
Marsh, Paul, 251
Masicampo, E.J., 255
Massey, Cade, 127-129
Matthew's story, housing market in Ft. Lauderdale, 215-217
McAdams, Scott, 30
medical decisions, shared decision making, 169
Medicare Part D, 173-175
medicine
    health insurance, 173-176
        Medicare Part D, 173-175
    patients, irrational thinking of, 167-171
mental accounting, 56
mergers, 189-190
Merrill Lynch, 202
    CEOs, 185
Microsoft, dividends, 29-30
Miller, Bill, 50
Miller, Merton, 27
misaggregation, 210
"Misery Is Not Miserly," 104

modern portfolio theory, 57
Modigliani, Franco, 27, 43
momentum, 83-86
    December effect, 86
    January effect, 86
    value investing, 87-89
money
    effect on the brain, 17-18
    mood and, 103-105
Montgomery, Richard, 143
mood, money and, 103-105
mortgage-backed securities,
    221-228
mortgages
    prepayment, 219
    securitization, 219-228
        ratings, 220
    subprime mortgages, 225
Moskowitz, Tobias, 87
Mullainathan, Sendhil, 40
munis (municipal bonds), 36-37
mutual funds, 47
    alpha, 48
    how our behavior damages
        investments, 51-53
    performance, 47-50
    returns-chasing behavior, 48
    trend chasing, 51

N

net stock issues anomaly, 77
neuroscience, 17
New Century Financial, 228
Newhouse, Joseph, 175
NFL draft, 125-126
    "the chart," 126-129
NFL Players Association,
    financial planning, 123
NFL Scouting Combine, 126
NINJA mortgages (no job verifi-
    cation, no income verification,
    no asset verification), 224
Nisbett, Richard, 249

Northern Rock, 229
Novemsky, Nathan, 100
Nudge, 137
nudges, behavioral economics, 257

O

O'Neal, Stanley, 202
Odean, Terry, 21-23
oil, 15
over-thinking, 131-134
overconfidence, 99, 214
    CEOs, 189-192

P

patients
    irrational thinking, 167-171
    shared decision making, 169
Paulson, Jr., Henry M., 240-245
Pedersen, Lasse Heje, 87-89, 230
Pelton, Robert Young, 61-62
performance, mutual funds, 47-50
persistence, 50
    alpha, 49
personal security, 151-153
    threat assessments, 152
Peyer, Urs, 81
Pfeiffer, Eckhard, 190
Pick-a-Pay, 157
Plott, Charlie, 207
portfolios, 55-56
    401(k)s, 55
    diversification, 57
    modern portfolio theory, 57
    multiple portfolios, 58
    postmodern portfolio theory,
        57-59
postmodern portfolio theory,
    57-59
Potchen, James, 98
predisposition to get-even-itis, 22
prepayment of mortgages, 219
Prince, Charles, 239

printers (computers), shrouded prices, 160
Prospect Theory, 99-102
pump and dump, 225

Q-R

questionnaires, risk tolerance, 63-64

radiology, 98
Rafter, Patrick, 133
Rajan, Raghuram, 227
Ranieri, Lou, 221, 227, 232
ratings agencies, 223
ratings of mortgage securities, 220
Rayner, Sharon, 155
Reagan, Nancy, 170
Redelmeier, Donald, 177
redlining, 217
reference points, disposition effect, 24
Regev, Tomer, 84
regret, 114
regulation, 19, 241-245, 263
    fire code regulation, 18
Regulation Z, 156
representative heuristics, 97
retirement
    annuities, 42-45
    investment versus consumption, 39-42
retirement calculators, 165
returns-chasing behavior, 47
riches to rags stories, football, 123
risk, longevity, 44
risk tolerance, 62
    identifying your true tolerance for financial risk, 64-65
    investing and, 62
    questionnaires, 63-64
Romer, Christina, 121
Romer, David, 120
Runyon, Damon, 112

S

sad people, money and, 104
Salomon Brothers, 221
Sampras, Pete, 133
Samuelson, Paul, 192
Sass, Steven, 164
Schoar, Antoinette, 183
Schwartz, Robert, 30
SEC, leverage, 240
securitization, 218-228
    ratings, 220
security, personal, 151
self-focus, 104
self-interest, 235
Shafir, Eldar, 64
shared decision making, 169
Shefrin, Hersh, 22, 106, 254
Sherman, Jim, 114
Shiller, Robert, 106, 227
Shin, Hyun, 232
shrouded prices, 159-162
Simon, Herbert, 106
"simplified" rules of thumb, 133
skepticism, 16
skin in the game, 199
Slovic, Paul, 106
snap judgments, 3, 148
    interest rates (credit cards), 158-159
    Social Security, 163-165
Social Security
    snap judgments, 163-165
    survivor benefits, 164
sounds, bids and asks, 210
speeding tickets, 180
Sports Illustrated, 192
Stang, Harry, 148
Stanovich, Keith, 5
Statman, Meir, 22, 55, 106-107
Staunton, Mike, 251
Stein, Jeremy, 80
Stewart, Martha, 194
Stiglitz, Joseph, 242

stock analysts, 67-71
stocks, timing, 77-81
Stranahan, Frank, 214
Stranahan House, 213
strategic inflection points, 184
strategic styles, CEOs, 183-186
subprime mortgages, 225
Sugg, Ron, 155
Sunbeam CEOs, 186
Sunstein, Cass, 137
superstar CEOs, 192-194
survivor benefits, Social Security, 164
Switzerland, health insurance, 176
System 1, 6-8
System 2, 6-8

T

taxes, financial advisors, 252
Templeton, John, 76
tennis, over-thinking, 131-134
Thain, John, 202-203
Thaler, Richard, 106, 127, 137, 258
theory, catering, 30
threat assessments, personal security, 152
Time Warner, 79
timing stocks, 77-81
toxic waste, 220
traffic jams, 178-179
tranches, 220
transparency in banking system, 244

trend chasing mutual funds, 51
True, Marion, 147-148
trusting your gut, 91-92
    volatility, 92
truth in lending, 156
Tversky, Amos, 96

U–V

U.S. financial crisis, 261-263
U.S. stocks, momentum, 88
Ubel, Peter, 170
universal default, 157
utility, 41

value investing, 73-76
    momentum, 87-89
value proposition, 74-75
Vermaelen, Theo, 78
volatility, trusting your gut, 92

W–Z

Wahal, Sunil, 130
Wall Street CEOs, 199-203
Welch, Jack, 181
Wolfers, Justin, 109
Womack, Kent, 68
women, Social Security, 164
Wonderlic, 127
Wrobel, Marian V., 40
Wurgler, Jeff, 28-31

Zinman, Jonathan, 158